Funded by the EU-China Managers Exchange and Training Programme
中国—欧盟经理人交流培训项目资助

Winning in China
— Business Chinese

 在中国 基础篇1 Basic 1

——商务汉语系列教程

● 编委会主任　王正富

● 编委会委员　曹红月　王福明　韩维春　季　瑾　李英海

● 主编　季　瑾

● 编者（按姓氏笔画顺序排列）

王会凤　余　瑛　季　瑾　崔艳蕾　梁　华

 北京语言大学出版社
BEIJING LANGUAGE AND CULTURE
UNIVERSITY PRESS

图书在版编目（CIP）数据

赢在中国：商务汉语系列教程. 基础篇. 1 / 季瑾
主编；王会凤等编著. —北京：北京语言大学出版社，
2010.6
ISBN 978-7-5619-2784-7

Ⅰ.①赢…　Ⅱ.①季…②王…　Ⅲ.①商务－汉语－
对外汉语教学－教材　Ⅳ.①H195.4

中国版本图书馆 CIP 数据核字（2010）第 099282 号

封面图片来源：**getty**images

书　　名：赢在中国——商务汉语系列教程·基础篇1
英文翻译：赵瑞华
责任印制：汪学发

出版发行：北京语言大学出版社
社　　址：北京市海淀区学院路 15 号　　　邮政编码：100083
网　　址：www. blcup. com
电　　话：发行部　82303650/3591/3651
　　　　　编辑部　82303647
　　　　　读者服务部　82303653/3908
　　　　　网上订购电话　82303668
　　　　　客户服务信箱　service@ blcup. net
印　　刷：北京联兴盛业印刷股份有限公司
经　　销：全国新华书店

版　　次：2010 年 6 月第 1 版　2010 年 6 月第 1 次印刷
开　　本：889 毫米 ×1194 毫米　1/16　印张：10
字　　数：230 千字
书　　号：ISBN 978-7-5619-2784-7/H·10158
定　　价：35.00 元

凡有印装质量问题，本社负责调换。电话：82303590

目 录
CONTENTS

语音介绍 Pronunciation	1

第一单元 UNIT 1	认识你很高兴 Nice to Meet You	打招呼 Greetings

注释 Notes：

1. "你好！"

2. 汉语的语序：主语 ＋ 动词 ＋ 宾语

   The basic order of the main elements of a Chinese sentence:

   Subject＋Verb＋Object

3. "是"字句 The "是"-sentence

4. 特指疑问句 The special question

5. 中国人的名字 Chinese names

6. 用"吗"的是非疑问句 The yes-or-no question with "吗"

7. 结构助词"的" The structural particle "的"

8. "有"字句（1） The "有"-sentence (1)

注释 Notes：

1. "您"

2. "您贵姓?"

3. 用"呢"的省略问句 The abbreviated question with "呢"

4. "欢迎……"

5. "再见！"

第二单元 UNIT 2　你是哪国人 Which country are you from　介绍自己 Introducing yourself

第三单元 UNIT 3 你在哪儿工作 谈工作
Where do you work Talking about one's job

编写说明

《赢在中国——商务汉语系列教程·基础篇》共三册，每册包括课文、生词、注释、练习和生词总表等几个部分。

（1）课文

课文以几位海外商务人士参与商务活动为主线，尽可能展示真实的社会生活场景。课文以情景对话的形式来传达社会生活信息及商务知识。

（2）生词

每册教材共有 300 个左右的生词，每个词语均配有拼音和英文翻译。

（3）注释

本教材的语法教学是为实用交际服务的，因此不单设语法模块，而是将语法安排在课文的注释中，相对弱化语法项目的讲解；而且，语法配合话题的需要，需要什么学什么，学什么讲什么，尽可能以例句和通俗的表述来展现语法，使学习者一看就懂，一学就会。此外，注释中除语法解释外，还有习惯用法、口语中的常用语、文化知识、商务常识等方面的介绍。

本教材参照国家汉办 2008 年最新颁布的《国际汉语教学通用课程大纲》中的《常用汉语语法项目分级表》，涵盖其中 1~5 级的绝大部分语法项目。其中 1~3 级全部覆盖，4 级仅一个量词"趟"没学，5 级语法中的"复句"一项也介绍了因果、转折、假设三种复句的基本形式和关联词语。本书突出集中强化的特色，增加了单位时间的学习效率。

（4）练习

练习包括机械操练、结构功能训练和商务交际训练三部分。练习类型各课基本一致，题型基本固定，前后练习统一，体现出训练的系统性。有时根据语言点的不同，题型略有差别。

每一课练习的前四项均为生词及课文朗读，目的在于通过语音上的机械强化，既解决学习者的语音问题，又帮助学习者在语音累积中获得语感。

结构功能训练是为学习者熟悉、掌握教材中的汉语词汇和句型而设计的。此部分练习不追求难度，如"替换练习"重在拓宽学习者的词汇视野、增加他们的语用信息，所以将示范的句型拆分开来，并列举出其他的使用情况，降低了难度。

练习的重点是商务交际训练，这主要体现在"完成任务"的练习中。我们设计了任务目标，既让学习者学以致用，调动自身已积累的语言能力来实战演练，也让学习者在"做中学"，培养学生在真实交际环境中的商务汉语交际能力，实现教学任务和现实世界社会经济生活的结合。

（5）教学建议

　　《基础篇》分为三册，周学习时间为 4~6 课时的普通教学班级可以一学期学习一册。对于学习时间集中的班级，如每周学习时间在 12 课时或以上的，可以一学期学完三册。本教材既可用于普通班的学习，也可用于强化性的学习；既可用于较长的完整学期的学习，也可用于周期性的短期学习。

　　本教材信息量大，内容分布广，练习设计具有一定的弹性，在教学过程中，可根据学习者的实际水平和教学安排灵活掌握。比如在"完成任务"的训练中，任务的要求可以富于弹性，对于水平高的学习者，可以让他们多完成一些任务，要求更多一些；而对于水平相对低一些的学习者，则可以降低要求，少完成一些任务或者将任务简化。

　　另外，建议学习者充分利用随书附赠的录音光盘，每次学习后至少能够听一遍，有时间再看着书听一遍。最好每天听一遍课文录音，每周至少能够听两次录音。这样可以帮助学习者强化听力，培养语感，从而综合提升听说的能力。

　　教材中如有任何不当之处，敬请读者予以指正，以便进一步修订。

对外经济贸易大学　季瑾

2010年3月于惠园

Preface

Winning in China—Business Chinese (Basic) (hereinafter referred to as *Basic*) consists of three textbooks. Each of them includes texts, new words, notes, exercises and a vocabulary list.

(1) Texts

Depicting the business activities of several businessmen from overseas, the texts reveal the real social life. Situational dialogues are presented in the texts to convey information on social life and to introduce business knowledge.

(2) New words

There are more than 300 new words in each textbook. *Pinyin* and English translation are provided for each of them.

(3) Notes

As grammar is taught for the purpose of communication in this set of textbooks, it is presented as "Notes" in each lesson rather than a separate section and taught based on the needs of topics with less emphasis. Grammatical points are explained with example sentences and colloquial expressions as much as possible in order for students to understand them without difficulty. Besides the grammatical explanations provided in the "Notes", idioms, colloquial expressions, cultural knowledge as well as general business knowledge are also introduced.

With reference to the *Grading List of Frequently Used Chinese Grammatical Items in Syllabus for International Chinese Teaching* issued by *Hanban* in 2008, the three textbooks of *Basic* cover the majority of the grammatical items of Grade 1~5. It covers all the grammatical items of the first four grades with the only exception of the measure word "趟" in Grade 4. The three basic compound sentence forms listed in Grade 5, i.e. the compound sentences of cause/effect, transition and assumption, as well as conjunctives are also introduced. The books feature intensive language training and improved efficiency of learning.

(4) Exercises

Exercises are of three types, pronunciation drills, exercises of language structures and functions, and business communication practice. The systematization of the practice is embodied by the facts that the types of exercises in each lesson are basically the same, and so are the types of questions, except for some exercises with slightly different types of questions due to the variation of language points.

The first four exercises in each lesson are reading aloud the new words and the texts with the aims to solve students' problems in pronunciation and to help them develop their sense of language through

intensive training in pronunciation.

Exercises of language structures and functions are designed to help students familiarize themselves with Chinese vocabulary and sentence patterns in the textbooks and learn to use them. These exercises are not meant to be difficult. For example, "Substitution drills" play an important role to enlarge students' vocabulary and provide them with more information on the usages of the language. Example sentence patterns are broken into several parts, and their other usages are listed so as to lower the degree of difficulty.

Training in business communication is the focus of the exercises, which can be seen in the exercise of "Completing the tasks". The objectives of a task are clearly defined and students are to use the language skills they have learned in practice and to learn the language while using it. The purpose is to develop students' communicative skills for business in a real communication environment by integrating learning of the language with real social and economic life.

(5) Suggestions for teaching

Basic consists of three books. One book could be finished in one semester for an ordinary class with 4~6 class hours per week. For those programs devoting more time in teaching, such as 12 class hours or more per week, three books can be finished in one semester. This set of books can be used either for an ordinary Chinese course or for an intensive Chinese training program, which means it can be used either for a long-term or a short-term Chinese program.

This set of textbooks is highly informative with a wide range of teaching materials and flexibly-designed exercises. It can be easily modified in teaching to respond to the level of students and the teaching arrangement. For example, when doing the exercise of "Completing the tasks", the task requirement could be varied. Advanced students may be encouraged to do more tasks with higher difficulty, while students of lower level may be asked to do less or easier ones.

In addition, I suggest that students make full use of the attached CD. They should listen to the CD at least once after each lesson and listen to it again while reading the book if they have time. It would be better if they listen to the recording of the text every day and listen to the recording at least twice a week. It will help them strengthen their listening skill, develop their sense of language and enhance their speaking skill.

Any suggestions for improvement of the book are highly welcomed.

Ji Jin,

University of International Business and Economics

At Hui Garden in March 2010

词类简称表
Abbreviations of parts of speech

缩写 Abbreviations	英文全称 Parts of speech in English	词类名称 Parts of speech in Chinese	拼音 Parts of speech in *pinyin*
Adj	Adjective	形容词	xíngróngcí
Adv	Adverb	副词	fùcí
AP	Aspect Particle	动态助词	dòngtài zhùcí
Conj	Conjunction	连词	liáncí
IE	Idiom Expression	习惯用语	xíguàn yòngyǔ
Int	Interjection	叹词	tàncí
LN	Locality Noun	方位词	fāngwèicí
M	Measure Word	量词	liàngcí
MdPt	Modal Particle	语气助词	yǔqì zhùcí
N	Noun	名词	míngcí
Nu	Numeral	数词	shùcí
Ono	Onomatopoeia	象声词	xiàngshēngcí
OpV	Optative Verb	能愿动词	néngyuàn dòngcí
PN	Proper Noun	专有名词	zhuānyǒu míngcí
Pr	Pronoun	代词	dàicí
Pref	Prefix	词头	cítóu
Prep	Preposition	介词	jiècí
Pt	Particle	助词	zhùcí
PW	Place Word	地点词	dìdiǎncí
Q	Quantifier	数量词	shùliàngcí
QPr	Question Pronoun	疑问代词	yíwèn dàicí
QPt	Question Particle	疑问助词	yíwèn zhùcí
StPt	Structural Particle	结构助词	jiégòu zhùcí
Suf	Suffix	词尾	cíwěi
TW	Time Word	时间词	shíjiāncí
V	Verb	动词	dòngcí
V//O	Verb-object Compound	离合词	líhécí

语法术语简称表
Abbreviations of grammatical terms

缩写 Abbreviations	英文全称 Grammatical terms in English	语法术语 Grammatical terms in Chinese	拼音 Grammatical terms in *pinyin*
S	Subject	主语	zhǔyǔ
P	Predicate	谓语	wèiyǔ
O	Object	宾语	bīnyǔ
Attr	Attribute	定语	dìngyǔ
A	Adverbial	状语	zhuàngyǔ
Comp	Complement	补语	bǔyǔ
NP	Noun Phrase	名词短语	míngcí duǎnyǔ
VP	Verbal Phrase	动词短语	dòngcí duǎnyǔ
PP	Prepositional Phrase	介词短语	jiècí duǎnyǔ
V O	Verb-object Phrase	动宾短语	dòng-bīn duǎnyǔ
	Declarative Sentence	陈述句	chénshùjù
	Interrogative Sentence	疑问句	yíwènjù
	Affirmative Sentence	肯定句	kěndìngjù
	Negative Sentence	否定句	fǒudìngjù
	General Interrogative Sentence	一般疑问句	yìbān yíwènjù
	Special Interrogative Sentence	特殊疑问句	tèshū yíwènjù
	Yes-or-no Question	是非疑问句	shìfēi yíwènjù
	Affirmative and Negative Question	正反疑问句	zhèngfǎn yíwènjù

主要人物介绍
Introduction of the main characters

Kǎ'ěr	Kāng Àilì	Lǐ Míngming	Zhāng Yuǎn
卡尔	**康爱丽**	**李明明**	**张远**
Karl Hofmann	**Alice Clement**	**Li Mingming**	**Zhang Yuan**

卡　尔——男，德国人，欧盟经理人；

康爱丽——女，法国人，欧盟经理人；

李明明——女，中国人，对外经济贸易大学国贸专业本科三年级学生；

张　远——男，中国人，对外经济贸易大学MBA二年级学生。

　　康爱丽、卡尔都是来北京接受汉语培训的欧盟经理人，李明明和张远是他们在对外经济贸易大学认识的朋友。

Ka'er—Karl Hofmann, male, a German manager from the European Union;

Kang Aili—Alice Clement, female, a French manager from the European Union;

Li Mingming—female, a Chinese junior majoring in International Trade at University of International Business and Economics;

Zhang Yuan—male, a Chinese MBA sophomore at University of International Business and Economics.

　　Both Kang Aili (Alice) and Ka'er (Karl) are managers from the European Union who came to Beijing for the training of Chinese language. Li Mingming and Zhang Yuan are their friends at University of International Business and Economics.

语音介绍
Pronunciation

■■■ 一、音节　**Syllables**

汉语的音节包括声母、韵母和声调三个部分。现代汉语普通话有 21 个声母、38 个韵母、4 个声调。声母在前，韵母在后，声调在韵母上。但有的音节只有韵母，没有声母。例如：

Chinese syllables include three parts: initials, finals and tones. There are twenty-one initials, thirty-eight finals and four tones in modern Mandarin Chinese. The initial goes first, and then the finals, with the tonal mark putting above the final. However, in some syllables, there is not an initial, but only a final. For example,

声母 Initial	韵母 Final	声调 Tone	音节 Syllable
b	a	ˉ	bā
p	o	ˊ	pó
m	i	ˇ	mǐ
f	u	ˋ	fù
/	ai	ˋ	ài

声母：音节开头的辅音。

Initial: It is the consonant at the beginning of a syllable.

韵母：音节中声母后面的部分。

Final: It follows the initial in a syllable.

声调：音节在发音时声音高低升降的变化。

Tone: It refers to the change of the pitch when the syllable is pronounced.

★ 小提示　**Tips**：

（1）声母和韵母拼合比较好的办法是"前音轻短后音重，两音相连猛一碰"。

A better way to combine the initial and final is to "pronounce the preceding sound (initial) lightly and shortly while the following sound emphatically, and when the two sounds meet, make a bump".

（2）普通话声母韵母拼合总表（见附 2）中的空白部分表示声母不能和这些韵母拼合。

The blank area in the *Table of the combinations of initials and finals in Mandarin Chinese* (see Appendix 2) indicates that these initials cannot be combined with those finals.

二、声母 Initials

声母表 Table of initials

发音方法 Manners of Articulation 发音部位 Places of Articulation	塞音 Stops		塞擦音 Affricates		鼻音 Nasals	边音 Lateral	擦音 Fricatives	
	不送气 Unaspirated	送气 Aspirated	不送气 Unaspirated	送气 Aspirated	浊 Voiced	浊 Voiced	清 Voiceless	浊 Voiced
上唇/下唇 Upper Lip/ Lower Lip	b [p]	p [p']			m [m]			
上齿/下唇 Upper Teeth/ Lower Lip							f [f]	
舌尖/上齿背 Tip of Tongue/ Upper Back of Teeth			z [ts]	c [ts']			s [s]	
舌尖/上齿龈 Tip of Tongue/ Upper Gum	d [t]	t [t']			n [n]	l [l]		
舌尖/硬腭前部 Tip of Tongue/ Front of Hard Palate			zh [tʂ]	ch [tʂ']			sh [ʂ]	r [z]
舌面前部/硬腭中部 Front of Tongue/ Middle of Hard Palate			j [tɕ]	q [tɕ']			x [ɕ]	
舌面后部/软腭 Back of Tongue/ Soft Palate	g [k]	k [k']					h [x]	

三、韵母 Finals

韵母表 Table of finals

	-i [ɿ] [ʅ]	i [i]	u [u]	ü [y]
单元音韵母 **Simple-Vowel Finals**	ɑ [A]			
	o [o]			
	e [ɤ]			
	er [ɚ]			
复元音韵母 **Compound-Vowel Finals**	ɑi [ai]	iɑ [iA]	uɑ [uA]	üe [yɛ]
	ei [ei]	ie [iɛ]	uo [uo]	
	ɑo [au]	iɑo [iɑu]	uɑi [uai]	
	ou [ou]	iou [iou]	uei [uei]	
鼻音韵母 **Nasal Finals**	ɑn [an]	iɑn [iɛn]	uɑn [uan]	üɑn [yɛn]
	en [ən]	in [in]	uen [uən]	ün [yn]
	ɑng [ɑŋ]	iɑng [iɑŋ]	uɑng [uɑŋ]	
	eng [əŋ]	ing [iŋ]	ueng [uəŋ]	
	ong [uŋ]	iong [yŋ]		

★ **注意 Notes:**

1. 字母 i 代表 3 种不同的发音，即：

   i represents three different pronunciations:

   i [i]: e.g. yī   -i [ɿ]: e.g. zī   -i [ʅ]: e.g. zhī

2. i 行的韵母，前面没有声母时，i 改为 y，写成：

   When there is not an initial in the front, the final i is changed into y, such as:

   yi   ya   ye   yao   you   yan   yin   yang   ying   yong

   u 行的韵母，前面没有声母时，u 改为 w，写成：

   When there is not an initial in the front, the final u is changed into w, such as:

   wu   wa   wo   wai   wei   wan   wen   wang   weng

   ü 行的韵母，前面没有声母时，ü 改为 y，写成：

   When there is not an initial in the front, the final ü is changed into y, such as:

   yu   yue   yuan   yun

3. 韵母 iou、uei、uen 的省写：为了使拼写简单，《汉语拼音方案》规定，iou、uei、uen 前面加声母的时候，写成 iu、ui、un。例如：

Abbreviations of the finals iou, uei, and uen. In order to simplify the spelling, *The Scheme for the Chinese Phonetic Alphabet* stipulates: if initials are preceded, iou, uei, and uen are abbreviated respectively as iu, ui, and un, such as:

niú　　guī　　lún

当它们不跟声母相拼（即自成音节）时就不能省略，要写成 y、w 开头。例如：

When not spelled with the initials, i.e., they form syllables on their own, they cannot be abbreviated but should still start with y or w, such as:

yōu　　wēi　　wēn

四、声调　Tones

1. 现代汉语普通话的音节有 4 个声调：一声（55）、二声（35）、三声（214）、四声（51）。此外，还有一种现象是轻声，不标调，声音短而轻。例如：

There are four tones in modern Mandarin Chinese: the 1st tone (its tone pitch is 55), the 2nd tone (its tone pitch is 35), the 3rd tone (its tone pitch is 214), and the 4th tone (its tone pitch is 51). Besides, there is a neutral tone without a tone mark. It is short and gentle, such as:

妈 mā　　麻 má　　马 mǎ　　骂 mà　　吗 ma

2. 声调特点：一声平、二声扬、三声拐弯、四声降。

Characteristics of the four tones: The 1st tone is flat; the 2nd tone is a rising tone; the 3rd tone starts at a low pitch and then rises; and the 4th tone is a falling tone.

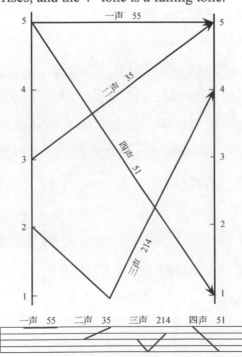

3. 标调顺序：标调要按照 ɑ、o、e、i、u、ü 的顺序，如 ɑo 的声调标在 ɑ 上，uo 的声调标在 o 上。

The tone mark sequence: A tone mark is placed in the sequence of ɑ, o, e, i, u, and ü. For example, the tone mark is placed above ɑ in ɑo and o in uo.

4. 特殊情况：Special cases:

（1）调号标在 i 的上面时，i 上的小点要省去。例如：

When a tone mark is placed above i, the dot in i is omitted. For example,

yī   xīng   duī   guī

（2）i、u 在一起时，声调标在后面，即 iu、ui 的调都应标在后一个字母上。例如：

When i and u appear together, the tone mark is placed above the latter one, i.e., the tone mark is placed on the latter final in iu and ui. For example,

qiū   duī   jiū   kuī

（3）ü 在 j、q、x 后要去掉两点，另外，在零声母音节（yu）中，也要去掉 ü 上两点。但是跟声母 n、l 相拼的时候，ü 上两点不可省略。例如：

The two dots in ü are omitted if it follows j, q, and x. Besides, the two dots in ü in the zero initial syllable (yu) are also omitted. However, the two dots in ü are not omitted if it is spelled with n and l. For example,

nǚ   lǚ

因为 j、q、x 不能跟 u 开头的韵母相拼，所以不用担心 ü 会与 u 相混。如 ju、que、xuɑn 中的 u 都是 ü 省略了两点。

Since j, q, and x are not spelled together with the finals starting with u, we don't need to worry that ü and u might be mixed up. For example, u in ju, que, and xuɑn is actually ü with the dots omitted.

★ **小提示　A Tip：**

ü 见 j、q、x、y，脱帽行个礼。

When meeting j, q, x, and y, ü always takes off the hat, bowing and saluting.

5. 变调：汉语中，在实际说话时会有一些变调的情况，比如两个三声在一起时，前一个音节要读得像二声。例如：

Tonal changes: In Chinese, tonal changes often happen in daily conversation. For instance, when there are two consecutive 3rd tones, the tone of the first syllable becomes a 2nd tone. For example,

nǐ hǎo ⟶ ní hǎo   hěn hǎo ⟶ hén hǎo

■■■ 五、隔音符号 Syllable-dividing mark

当 a、o、e 开头的音节连接在其他音节后面的时候，音节界限容易混淆，可以用隔音符号（'）隔开。例如："西安"写成 Xī'ān，"方案"写成 fāng'àn，"金额"写成 jīn'é。

When the syllables starting with a, o, e follow other syllables, the division of the syllables are easily confused. Therefore, we can use the syllable-dividing mark to separate them. For example, "西安" is written as Xī'ān, "方案" is written as fāng'àn, and "金额" is written as jīn'é.

如果第二个音节的开头是辅音，那么不必使用隔音符号。如"发难（fānàn）"就不必写成 fā'nàn。

If the second syllable starts with a consonant, the syllable-dividing mark is not needed. For example, "发难" is fānàn, not fā'nàn.

● 小窍门：看到分词连写的汉语拼音注音时，怎么判断和区分音节呢？

A tip: If placing *pinyin* for Chinese phrases, how can we separate the syllables?

音节中的辅音字母"靠后不靠前"，即一个辅音字母如果前后都有元音字母，这个辅音应当跟后面的元音字母连成音节。例如："他们"（tāmen）中，辅音字母 m 前后都有元音字母，m 应跟后面的元音字母 en 连成音节；而"谈话"（tánhuà）的辅音字母 n 后面没有元音字母，因此 n 跟前面的元音字母连成音节，而 h 跟后面的 ua 连成音节。

The consonant in a syllable links with the vowel after it, not the one before it. That is, if there is a vowel both before and after a consonant, the consonant links with the vowel that follows it to make up a syllable. For example, there is a vowel both before and after the third letter m in "他们" (tāmen), therefore, m links with the vowel en after it to make up a syllable. However, there is no vowel after the third letter n in "谈话" (tánhuà); therefore, n links with the vowel before it to form a syllable, but h links with ua following it to form a syllable.

■■■ 六、整体认读音节 The holistic syllable

汉语中有一些整体认读音节，不能拼读，只能直呼。例如：

There are some holistic syllables in Chinese that are not pronounced separately, but are pronounced as a whole, such as:

zhi chi shi ri zi ci si yi wu yu ye yue yuan yin yun ying

■■■ 七、字母的大写 Rules of capitalization

1. 句子或诗行开头的字母要大写。例如：

The initial letter of a sentence or a line in a poem is capitalized. For example,

Nín guìxìng?（您贵姓？）

Chuáng qián míng yuè guāng,（床前明月光，）

Yí shì dìshang shuāng.（疑是地上霜。）

Jǔ tóu wàng míng yuè,（举头望明月，）

Dī tóu sī gùxiāng.（低头思故乡。）

2. 专有名词的第一个字母要大写。例如：

The first letter of a proper noun is capitalized. For example,

Zhōngguó Rìbào（中国日报）

3.汉语的人名按姓和名分写，姓和名的开头字母要大写。例如：

A Chinese name is written separately with the first letters of both the surname and the given name capitalized. For example,

Lǐ Bái（李白）　　　Kāng Àilì（康爱丽）

4. 标题可以全部大写，也可以每个词开头的字母大写。有时为了美观，可以省略声调符号。例如：

All the letters of a title can be capitalized, or only the first letter of each word is capitalized. Sometimes, to be artistic, the tone marks can be omitted. For example,

FAZHAN JINGJI, JIANSHE ZHONGGUO（发展经济，建设中国）

Fāzhǎn Jīngjì, Jiànshè Zhōngguó

附1：发音器官图

Appendix 1：The illustration of speech organs

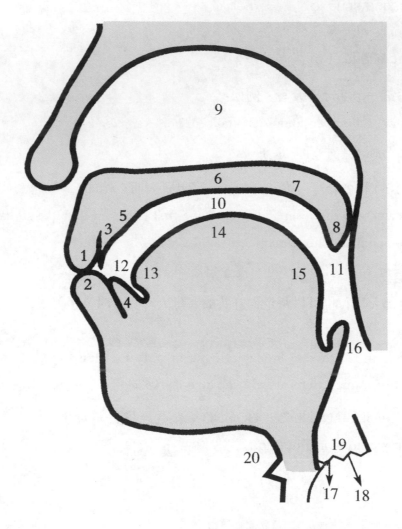

1. 上唇　Upper Lip

2. 下唇　Lower Lip

3. 上齿　Upper Teeth

4. 下齿　Lower Teeth

5. 齿龈　Gingiva, Gum

6. 硬腭　Hard Palate

7. 软腭　Soft Palate

8. 小舌　Uvula

9. 鼻腔　Nasal Cavity

10. 口腔　Oral Cavity

11. 咽腔　Pharynx Cavity

12. 舌尖　Tip of Tongue

13. 舌叶　Tongue Blade

14. 舌面前和舌面中　Front of the Tongue and Middle of the Tongue

15. 舌面后（舌根）　Back of Tongue

16. 会厌软骨　Cartilago Epiglottica

17. 肺　Lung

18. 气管　Air Tube

19. 声带　Vocal Cords

20. 喉头　Throat

认识你很高兴
Nice to Meet You

课文 Text	题目 Title	注释 Notes
一	你叫什么名字 What's your name	1. "你好！" 2. 汉语的语序：主语 + 动词 + 宾语 The basic order of the main elements of a Chinese sentence: Subject+Verb+Object 3. "是"字句　The "是"-sentence 4. 特指疑问句 The special question 5. 中国人的名字　Chinese names 6. 用"吗"的是非疑问句 The yes-or-no question with "吗" 7. 结构助词"的"　The structural particle "的" 8. "有"字句（1） The "有"-sentence（1）
二	您贵姓 May I have your surname, please	1. "您" 2. "您贵姓？" 3. 用"呢"的省略问句 The abbreviated question with "呢" 4. "欢迎……" 5. "再见！"
三	请问，您是王经理吗 Excuse me, are you Manager Wang	1. "请问，……" 2. 句型："您是 +sb.+ 吗？" The sentence pattern："您是 +sb.+ 吗？" 3. "请 +V"

Nǐ Jiào Shénme Míngzi

你叫什么名字

What's your name

Kāng Àilì、Kǎ'ěr zài jiàoshì li chūcì jiànmiàn.

康爱丽、卡尔在教室里初次见面。

Alice and Karl are meeting in the classroom for the first time.

Kǎ'ěr: Nǐ hǎo!
● 卡尔：你好！
Karl: Hello!

Kāng Àilì: Nǐ hǎo!
○ 康爱丽：你好！
Alice: Hello!

Kǎ'ěr: Wǒ shì Kǎ'ěr. Nǐ jiào shénme míngzi?
● 卡尔：我是卡尔。你叫什么名字？
Karl: I am Karl. What's your name?

Kāng Àilì: Wǒ jiào Kāng Àilì.
○ 康爱丽：我叫康爱丽。
Alice: My name is Kang Aili (Alice Clement).

Kǎ'ěr: Zhè shì nǐ de Zhōngwén míngzi ma?

● 卡尔： 这是你的中文名字吗？

Karl: Is this your Chinese name?

Kāng Àilì: Shì de. Nǐ yǒu Zhōngwén míngzi ma?

○ 康爱丽： 是的。你有中文名字吗？

Alice: Yes. Do you have a Chinese name?

Kǎ'ěr: Yǒu. Kǎ'ěr shì wǒ de Déguó míngzi, yě shì wǒ de Zhōngwén míngzi.

● 卡尔： 有。卡尔是我的德国名字，也是我的中文名字。

Karl: Karl is my German name and Ka'er my Chinese name.

Kāng Àilì: Hěn gāoxìng rènshi nǐ!

○ 康爱丽： 很高兴认识你！

Alice: Nice to meet you!

Kǎ'ěr: Rènshi nǐ hěn gāoxìng!

● 卡尔： 认识你很高兴！

Karl: Nice to meet you, too!

生词	Shēngcí	**New Words**		
1. 你	nǐ	Pr	you
2. 叫	jiào	V	to call
3. 什么	shénme	QPr	what
4. 名字	míngzi	N	name
5. 好	hǎo	Adj	good
6. 我	wǒ	Pr	I, me
7. 是	shì	V	to be
8. 这	zhè	Pr	this
9. 的	de	StPt	*a possessive or modifying particle*
10. 中文	Zhōngwén	N	Chinese language
11. 吗	ma	QPt	*a particle*
12. 有	yǒu	V	to have
13. 也	yě	Adv	too, also

14.	很	hěn	Adv	very
15.	高兴	gāoxìng	Adj	happy
16.	认识	rènshi	V	to know

专有名词 Zhuānyǒu Míngcí　**Proper Nouns**

1.	卡尔	Kǎ'ěr	a person's name
2.	康爱丽	Kāng Àilì	a person's name
3.	德国	Déguó	Germany

注释　Zhùshì　**Notes**

1 你好！Hello!

中国人平常见面，不管是否认识都可以互相说"你好"，这和英文里"Hello"的用法一样。初次见面时，双方互相介绍完以后，都可以说"很高兴认识你（您）"，或者"认识你（您）很高兴"。这和英文里的"Nice to meet you"用法类似。

When Chinese people meet each other, no matter whether they know each other, they can say "你好", which is similar to "Hello" in English. When people meet each other for the first time, after introducing themselves, they say "很高兴认识你（您）", or "认识你（您）很高兴" to each other, which is similar to "Nice to meet you" in English.

2 我是卡尔。I am Karl. ／ 我叫康爱丽。My name is Kang Aili (Alice Clement).

汉语的语序是：主语＋动词＋宾语，这和英语类似。

The order of the main elements of a Chinese sentence: Subject+ Verb + Object. It is similar to English.

S	V	O
我	叫	康爱丽。
我	有	中文名字。

汉语的句子一般可以分为两个部分：主语部分和谓语部分；有六种句子成分：主语、谓语、宾语、定语、状语和补语。它们在句中的位置见下表：

A Chinese sentence can generally be divided into two parts, the subject and the predicate. Generally speaking, there are six sentence elements in a Chinese sentence: subject, predicate, object, attribute, adverbial and complement. The positions of these sentence elements in a sentence are shown in the following table:

主语部分 Subject part		谓语部分 Predicate part			
	主语 S		谓语动词 Predicative verb		宾语 O
定语 Attr	状语 A		补语 Comp	定语 Attr	

"我叫康爱丽"一句里包含三种句子成分："我"是主语，"叫"是谓语，"康爱丽"是宾语。

There are three elements in the sentence "我叫康爱丽"．"我"is the subject,"叫"is the predicate and"康爱丽"the object.

3 我是卡尔。I am Karl.

"是"字句。这是动词"是"作谓语动词的句型。"A 是 B"主要是表示判断，说明人或事物等于什么或者属于什么。

The "是"-sentence is a sentence pattern with "是" as the predicate. "A 是 B" mainly denotes a judgement, indicating that a person or thing equals to or belongs to something else.

"是"字句的否定形式是在"是"的前面加表示否定的副词"不（bù）"。如果句子中有副词"也"，"也"放在"是"的前面。例如：

The negative form of the "是"-sentence is to place the adverb "不" before "是". If there is the adverb "也" in the sentence, "也" is placed before "是". For example,

S	P		
	Adv	V（是）	N／NP
我			康爱丽。
卡尔			我的德国名字。
卡尔	也	是	我的中文名字。
我	不		康爱丽。
康爱丽	也不		中国人（Zhōngguó rén，Chinese）。

4 你叫什么名字？ **What's your name?**

特指疑问句。"什么"，疑问代词，表示疑问，可以问人或者事物。

In a special question, the interrogative pronoun "什么" is used to ask a question about persons or things.

汉语的特指问句和英文的特殊问句不一样，不用变换语序，只是用"什么"等一些表示疑问的词语来替换陈述句中被提问的部分，句末用表示疑问的问号（？）。例如：

In a special question in Chinese, in contrast to English, there is no change in the word order. A word indicating interrogation like "什么" is used to replace the part in a declarative sentence to be inquired with a question mark at the end of the sentence. For example,

	S	P	
		V	O
Sentence	我	叫	卡尔。
Question	你	叫	什么（名字）？

5 我叫康爱丽。 **My name is Kang Aili（Alice Clement）.**

中国人的名字是"姓＋名"，根据喜好，有的人的名字用两个字，有的人的名字只有一个字。例如：

A Chinese name is composed of a surname and a given name. The given name can be one character or two characters according to the preference. For example,

Surname（姓）	Given Name（名）
康	爱丽
李 (Lǐ)	明明（Míngming）
张 (Zhāng)	远 (Yuǎn)

6 这是你的中文名字吗？ **Is this your Chinese name?**

是非疑问句。"这是……吗"表示疑问。

The yes-or-no question. "这是……吗" is used to indicate interrogation.

汉语中，把表示疑问的语气助词"吗"放在陈述句的句末，把原句变成疑问句。听话人要作出肯定（"是"）或者否定（"不是"）的回答。例如：

In Chinese, a declarative sentence can be changed into an interrogative sentence by putting the interrogative particle "吗" at the end of the sentence. The listener expects an affirmative (Yes) or a negative (No) answer. For example,

		General interrogative sentence	
		Original sentence	Particle（吗）
这	是	你的中文名字	吗？
		你的书（shū, book）	
		你们（nǐmen, you）的教室（jiàoshì, classroom）	
你		卡尔	
		康爱丽	

7 这是你的中文名字吗？ **Is this your Chinese name?**

"的"，结构助词，常用在定语后，是定语的语法标志。它连接定语和它修饰的中心语，表示领属关系、修饰或限制关系。汉语中的定语一般放在中心语前，除连词、助词、叹词外，各种词语都能作定语。例如：

"的" is a structural particle often used after an attribute and serves as the grammatical marker for it. It links the attribute and the word it modifies, indicating the possessive, modifying or restrictive relationship. In Chinese, an attribute is usually used before the word it modifies. All the words can be used as attributes except conjunctions, auxiliaries and interjections. For example,

Attr	StPt（的）	Head word
你（N）	的	老师
学校（xuéxiào, school）（N）		公寓（gōngyù, apartment）
认识（V）		人
高兴（Adj）		事儿（shìr, thing）
他问（wèn, to ask）（clause）		问题（wèntí, question）

8 你有中文名字吗？ **Do you have a Chinese name?**

"有"字句。这里表示"拥有"的意思。肯定式为"A有B"；疑问式为"A有B吗"；否定式中用"没有（méiyǒu）"，为"A没有B"。例如：

The "有"-sentence. "有" means "have". Its affirmative form is "A 有 B", its interrogative form is "A 有 B 吗", and its negative form is "A 没有 B". For example,

S	V	O
我	有	中文名字。
你	有	中文名字吗？
我	没有	中文名字。

疑问句"你有……吗"和英文里"Do you have..."的用法类似。回答时可以用完整的句子，也可以简单地用"有"（肯定）或"没有"（否定）。例如：

The interrogative sentence "你有……吗" is similar to "Do you have..." in English. The answer can be a complete sentence, or simply "有" (yes) or "没有" (no) . For example,

疑问句 Interrogative sentence	你有中文名字吗？
肯定回答 Affirmative answer	我有中文名字。/有。
否定回答 Negative answer	我没有中文名字。/没有。

Nín Guìxìng
您贵姓
May I have your surname, please

Kāng Àilì hé Wáng lǎoshī zài jiàoshì li chūcì jiànmiàn.
康爱丽和王老师在教室里初次见面。
Alice and Mr. Wang are meeting in the classroom for the first time.

Kāng Àilì: Lǎoshī, nín hǎo!
● 康爱丽： 老师，您好！
Alice:　　Hello! Teacher.

Wáng lǎoshī: Nǐ hǎo!
○ 王老师： 你好！
Mr. Wang:　Hello!

Kāng Àilì: Nín guìxìng?
● 康爱丽： 您贵姓？
Alice:　　May I have your surname, please?

Wáng lǎoshī: Wǒ xìng Wáng. Nǐ ne?
○ 王老师： 我姓王。你呢？
Mr. Wang:　My surname is Wang, and yours?

Kāng Àilì: Wǒ xìng Kāng, wǒ jiào Kāng Àilì.
● 康爱丽： 我姓康，我叫康爱丽。
Alice:　　 Mine is Kang. My name is Kang Aili (Alice).

Wáng lǎoshī: Huānyíng nǐ lái Běijīng!
○ 王老师：　 欢迎你来北京！
Mr. Wang:　 Welcome to Beijing!

Kāng Àilì: Xièxie! Zàijiàn!
● 康爱丽： 谢谢！再见！
Alice:　　 Thank you. Goodbye!

Wáng lǎoshī: Zàijiàn!
○ 王老师：　 再见！
Mr. Wang:　 Goodbye!

生词　Shēngcí　New Words

1. 您	nín	Pr	you (respectful form)
2. 贵姓	guìxìng	N	(honorable) surname
3. 老师	lǎoshī	N	teacher
4. 姓	xìng	V/N	one's surname is… ; surname
5. 呢	ne	MdPt	*a modal particle*
6. 欢迎	huānyíng	V	to welcome
7. 来	lái	V	to come
8. 谢谢	xièxie	V	to thank
9. 再见	zàijiàn	V	goodbye
见	jiàn	V	to see

专有名词　Zhuānyǒu Míngcí　Proper Nouns

1. 王	Wáng	a surname
2. 康	Kāng	a surname
3. 北京	Běijīng	Beijing, the capital of China

注释 Zhùshì **Notes**

1 您好！Hello！

"您"。汉语中，用"您"表示对对方的尊敬，尤其是和上级、长辈，如老师、老板、父母说话时。初次见面，对同辈的人也可用"您"表示礼貌和尊重。

In Chinese, "您" is used to show respect to the other party, especially when talking to your superiors or seniors, such as your teacher, boss and parents, etc. When meeting your peers for the first time, "您" is also used to show your courtesy and respect.

2 您贵姓？May I have your surname, please？

初次见面，为了表示礼貌和尊重，询问别人的姓名时常用"您贵姓"、"您怎么称呼（Nín zěnme chēnghu）"，尤其是对年长的人和上级。对同辈或年轻、地位低的人，常用"你叫什么名字"。

When people meet for the first time, in order to show your courtesy and respect to the other party, especially to your superiors, "您贵姓"、"您怎么称呼（How should I address you）" are often used to ask their names. However, when the people you speak to is your peer, younger than or inferior to you, "你叫什么名字" is often used.

有时候也可以这样说："我是卡尔。你（您）是……？"前一句介绍自己的名字，后一句是省略的问句，用询问的语气，表示不知道对方的情况。

Sometimes, we can also say "我是卡尔。你（您）是……？" The first sentence is to give a self-introduction. The inquiring tone is used in the last sentence, and the omitting part indicates that the speaker doesn't know about him or her.

对这些不同问法的回答都可以是："我姓……"或"我叫……"。例如：

The answers to these questions can be "我姓……" or "我叫……". For example,

Question	Answer
您贵姓？ 您怎么称呼？	我姓……。 我叫……。 我是……。 康爱丽。
我叫/是卡尔，你叫什么名字？ 我叫/是卡尔，你呢？ 我是卡尔，你（您）是……？	我叫……。 我是……。 康爱丽。

3 你呢？And yours?

省略问句。"你呢"是说话人在说明了一个情况后问对方相同方面的问题时用的。在一定的语境中，用疑问代词的特指问句的疑问点可以省略，表示疑问的词语"呢"直接放在代词或名词后构成问句。例如：

It is an elliptical question used to ask the same question after giving an explanation. In certain context, what to be asked is omitted with the interrogative word "呢" placed directly after a pronoun or a noun. For example,

①A: 我姓王。你呢？（It means "你姓什么？"）

  B: 我姓康。

②A: 我叫卡尔。你呢？（It means "你叫什么名字？"）

  B: 我叫康爱丽。

4 欢迎你来北京！Welcome to Beijing!

在日常交际中，无论是对熟人还是陌生人，当你是主人，别人来到你的国家、城市、工作单位、学校、家等地方时，对来人表示欢迎时可以说"欢迎"、"欢迎，欢迎"或者"欢迎+短语"，以体现主人的礼貌和热情。例如：

In daily communication, if you are a host, when people, familiar or not, come to your country, city, work unit, school or home, you can say "欢迎"，"欢迎，欢迎"，or "欢迎 +phrase" to show your courtesy and hospitality. For example,

V（欢迎）		Phrase
欢迎	你来	北京。
		上海（Shànghǎi, one of the largest cities in China）。
		中国（Zhōngguó, China）。
		我的公司（gōngsī, company）。

5 再见！Goodbye!

"再见"，客套话，日常生活中告别时用，回答也是"再见"，类似英文里的"Goodbye"。除了"再见"，还可以用时间、地点等名词加上动词"见"来表示告别。例如：

"再见" is a daily expression of politeness used when people bid farewell to each other. It is equivalent to "Goodbye" in English. In addition, we also say goodbye by using "见" after a noun of time or place, etc. For example,

①A: 再见！

  B: 再见！

②A: 明天(míngtiān, tomorrow) 见！

  B: 再见！

③A: 北京见！

  B: 再见！

Qǐngwèn, Nín Shì Wáng Jīnglǐ ma

请问，您是王经理吗

Excuse me, are you Manager Wang

Kāng Àilì hé Wáng jīnglǐ yuēhǎo zài tā de gōngsī
jiànmiàn. Kāng Àilì zài jīnglǐ bàngōngshì kànjian yí wèi
nánshì. Zhè shì tāmen dì yī cì jiànmiàn.

康爱丽和王经理约好在他的公司见面。康爱丽看见
经理办公室里有一位男士。这是他们第一次见面。

Manager Wang has made an appointment with Alice to
meet each other in his company. Alice saw a gentleman in
the manager's office. This was the first time they meet.

Kāng Àilì: Qǐngwèn, nín shì Wáng jīnglǐ ma?

● 康爱丽：请问，您是王经理吗？

Alice:　　Excuse me, are you Manager Wang?

Wáng jīnglǐ:　Shì. Nín shì……?

○ 王经理：　　是。您是……？

Manager Wang: Yes, and you are...?

Kāng Àilì: Nín hǎo! Wǒ shì Kāng Àilì.

● 康爱丽：您好！我是康爱丽。

Alice:　　Hello! I am Kang Aili (Alice Clement).

Wáng jīnglǐ:　Nín hǎo! Huānyíng, huānyíng! Qǐng jìn!

○ 王经理：　　您好！欢迎，欢迎！请进！

Manager Wang: Hello! Welcome! Please come in.

21

生词 Shēngcí New Words

1.	请问	qǐngwèn	V	excuse me
2.	经理	jīnglǐ	N	manager
3.	请	qǐng	V	please
4.	进	jìn	V	to come in

注释 Zhùshì Notes

1 请问，您是王经理吗？ Excuse me, are you Manager Wang?

"请问"，用来询问一件事，一般直接放在问句前，引出问题，如问别人的姓名、问地点、问时间、打听事情，等等。例如：

"请问" is used before an interrogative sentence when asking a question, for example, asking for the name of the other party, the direction, time or other information, etc. For example,

V（请问），	Question
	您是王经理吗？
	你有中文名字吗？
请问，	您贵姓？
	厕所（cèsuǒ, restroom, toilet）在（zài, at, in, on）哪儿（nǎr, where）？

2 您是王经理吗？ Are you Manager Wang?

"您是 +sb.+ 吗"，这是说话人在不能确定对方就是自己认为的那个人时用的问句。如卡尔认为这个女生可能是康爱丽，但又不能确定时，可以说："你是康爱丽吗？"例如：

This sentence is used when the speaker is not sure whether the person is the right one. For example, if Karl thinks the girl might be Alice, but he isn't sure, then he can say "你是康爱丽吗？" For example,

Pr	V（是）	sb.	Qpt（吗）
您		王经理	
你		康爱丽	
他（tā, he）	是	卡尔	吗？
她（tā, she）		李明明（Lǐ Míngming, a person's name）	

3 请进！ **Please come in!**

"请"，礼貌用语，常常放在动词或短语前。例如：

In Chinese, "请" is a term of politeness and is often used before a verb or a phrase. For example,

请 + V	
请	进
	坐（zuò, to sit）
	听（tīng, to listen）

请 + VP	
请	喝茶（hē chá, to have some tea）
	吃水果（chī shuǐguǒ, to eat fruits）
	回答问题（huídá wèntí, to answer the question）

练习 Liànxí **Exercises**

一 跟读生词,注意发音和声调。
Read the new words after the teacher and pay attention to your pronunciation.

二 跟读课文,注意语音语调。
Read the texts after the teacher and pay attention to your pronunciation.

三 学生分组,分角色朗读课文一、二、三。
Divide the students into groups and read Texts 1, 2 & 3 in roles.

四 学生分组,不看书,分角色表演课文一、二、三。
Divide the students into groups and play the roles in Texts 1, 2 & 3 without referring to the book.

五 角色扮演。(提示:角色可以互换。)
Role play. (Note: the roles can be exchanged.)

请一名学生（A）站在班级的中央,大家一起拍手,拍 5 下后,由老师说出任意一名学生（B）的名字,学生 B 就走到 A 的对面,两人握手,然后完成下面的对话:

Ask a student, A, to stand in the middle of the class. The rest of the students clap their hands together for five times. And then the teacher calls the name of another student, B. Student B walks up to Student A. The two shake hands and complete the following dialogue.

学生 A	学生 B
你好!	……
你叫什么名字?	……
……	你叫什么名字?
再见!	……

六 替换练习。
Substitution drills.

① 我 是 卡尔。

你	康爱丽
卡尔	经理
康爱丽	老师
这	我的名字

② 你 有 中文名字 吗?

> 卡尔　　　　德国名字
>
> 康爱丽　　　书
>
> 他　　　　　名片 (míngpiàn, business card)
>
> 你　　　　　中国朋友 (péngyou, friend)
>
> 你　　　　　时间 (shíjiān, time)

③ 请问，您是王经理吗?

> 您有中文名字吗
>
> 您是卡尔吗
>
> 你叫什么名字
>
> 您贵姓

④ 卡尔 是 我的德国名字，也 是 我的中文名字。

> 明明　　我的朋友　　　　　　我的同事 (tóngshì, colleague)
>
> 康爱丽　经理　　　　　　　　学生 (xuésheng, student)
>
> 他　　　我的同学 (tóngxué, classmate)　我的朋友

七 用下面的词语组成句子。

Make sentences with the following words and expressions.

① 贵　您　姓

② 我　王　姓

③ 卡尔　是　我

④ 我　　康爱丽　　叫

⑤ 这　　的　　吗　　是　　中文名字　　你

⑥ 你　　中文名字　　吗　　有

⑦ 您　　很　　认识　　高兴

⑧ 您　　王经理　　请问　　是　　吗

 八 完成任务：请用课文中学过的词语和句子完成任务。
Complete the tasks: Please complete the tasks with the phrases and sentences you have learned in the texts.

课上完成（Classroom activity）：

由老师说出几个学生的名字，通过询问，在教室里找到这些同学。
After the teacher calls the names of several students, please find them through inquiry.

课后完成（Homework）：

1. 请去学生管理办公室或教师办公室找到老师让你找的人。
   Please find the person your teacher wants in the Student Management Office or the Teachers' office.

2. 请调查你的两位同学和至少一位老师的名字，然后在课堂上告诉大家。
   Please find out the names of two of your classmates and at least one of your teachers, and then tell their names to your classmates in class.

第二单元
UNIT 2
介绍自己
Introducing yourself

你是哪国人
Which country are you from

课文 Text	题目 Title	注释 Notes
一	你是哪国人 Which country are you from	1. 疑问代词"哪"　The interrogative pronoun "哪" 2. 洲名／国家／城市／地区＋"人" Name of a continent/country/city/area ＋"人" 3. 副词"都"　The adverb "都" 4. 第三人称单数"他／她" 　　The third person singular "他／她" 5. 是非疑问句的回答形式 　　The answering pattern to the yes-or-no question 6. 指示代词"那／这" 　　The demonstrative pronoun "那／这" 7. 量词"位"　The measure word "位" 8. 疑问代词"谁"　The interrogative pronoun "谁"
二	叫我明明吧 Please call me Mingming	1. 汉语的称谓　Forms of address in Chinese 2. "V＋一下" 3. 双宾语动词谓语句 　　The verbal predicate sentence with double objects 4. 语气助词"吧"　The modal particle "吧" 5. 量词"个"及"数词＋量词＋名词"结构 　　The measure word "个" and the structure 　　"Numeral ＋ Measure word ＋ Noun"
三	你住在哪儿 Where do you live	1. 疑问代词"哪儿" 　　The interrogative pronoun "哪儿" 2. 介词"在"(1)　The preposition "在"(1)

Nǐ Shì Nǎ Guó Rén
你是哪国人
Which country are you from

Zài xīn xuéqī de jùhuì shang.
在新学期的聚会上。
At the party of a new semester.

Kāng Àilì: Qǐngwèn, nǐ shì nǎ guó rén?
● 康爱丽: 请问，你是哪国人？
Alice:　　Excuse me, which country are you from?

Kǎ'ěr: Wǒ shì Déguó rén. Nǐ ne?
○ 卡尔：我是德国人。你呢？
Karl:　　I am from Germany. What about you?

Kāng Àilì: Fǎguó rén. Wǒmen dōu shì Ōuzhōu rén.
● 康爱丽: 法国人。我们都是欧洲人。
Alice:　　I am from France. We are both Europeans.

Kǎ'ěr zhǐzhe yí wèi nánshì wèn……
卡尔指着一位男士问……
Pointing to a man, Karl asks…

Kǎ'ěr: Tā yě shì Fǎguó rén ma?

● 卡尔： 他也是法国人吗？

Karl:　Is he French, too?

Kāng Àilì: Tā bú shì Fǎguó rén, shì Zhōngguó rén.

○ 康爱丽： 他不是法国人，是中国人。

Alice:　No, he isn't. He is Chinese.

Kǎ'ěr zhǐzhe yí wèi nǚshì wèn……

卡尔指着一位女士问……

Pointing to a lady, Karl asks...

Kǎ'ěr: Tā ne?

● 卡尔： 她呢？

Karl:　What about her?

Kāng Àilì: Tā yě shì Zhōngguó rén.

○ 康爱丽： 她也是中国人。

Alice:　She is also Chinese.

Kǎ'ěr: Nǐ rènshi tā ma?

● 卡尔： 你认识她吗？

Karl:　Do you know her?

Kāng Àilì: Rènshi.

○ 康爱丽： 认识。

Alice:　Yes, I do.

Kǎ'ěr zhǐzhe lìng yí wèi nǚshì wèn……

卡尔指着另一位女士问……

Pointing to another lady, Karl asks...

Kǎ'ěr: Nà wèi xiǎojie shì shéi?

● 卡尔： 那位小姐是谁？

Karl:　Who is that lady?

Kāng Àilì: Tā shì wǒ de péngyou, yě shì wǒ de fǔdǎo lǎoshī.

○ 康爱丽： 她是我的朋友，也是我的辅导老师。

Alice:　She is my friend and my tutor, too.

生词　Shēngcí　**New Words**

1. 哪	nǎ / něi	QPr	which
2. 国	guó	N	country, nation
3. 人	rén	N	person, people
4. 我们	wǒmen	Pr	we, us
5. 都	dōu	Adv	both, all
6. 他	tā	Pr	he, him
7. 她	tā	Pr	she, her
8. 那	nà / nèi	Pr	that
9. 位	wèi	M	*a polite measure word for people*
10. 小姐	xiǎojie	N	Miss, young lady
11. 谁	shéi / shuí	QPr	who, whom
12. 朋友	péngyou	N	friend
13. 辅导	fǔdǎo	V	to coach, to tutor

专有名词　Zhuānyǒu Míngcí　**Proper Nouns**

1. 法国	Fǎguó	France
2. 欧洲	Ōuzhōu	Europe
3. 中国	Zhōngguó	China

注释　Zhùshì　**Notes**

1 你是哪国人？ **Which country are you from?**

　　"哪"，疑问代词，和英语里的 which 类似。后面跟量词或数量词。根据后面数量词和名词的不同，"哪"可以询问人、事物、地点和时间等，这时口语里常说成"něi 或 nǎi"。单用的"哪"在口语里只说"nǎ"。例如：

"哪", an interrogative pronoun similar to "which" in English, is followed by a measure word or a quantifier. According to the quantifier and the noun it follows, "哪" can be used to ask about people, thing, place or time, etc. when it is pronounced as nĕi or nǎi in oral Chinese. However, when it is used separately, it is pronounced as nǎ. For example,

① 哪（一）位小姐是李明明？（问人 To ask about a person）

② 我们哪天 (tiān, day) 见？（问时间 To ask about time）

③ 你要哪本 (běn, *a measure word for books*) 书？（问事物 To ask about a thing）

2 **我是德国人。I am from Germany.**

汉语里，为表示一个人来自某个地方，常在他所属的洲、国家、城市的后面加上"人"。例如：

In Chinese, "人" is often used after a continent, a country, or a city to denote where a person comes from. For example,

① 欧洲——欧洲人

② 中国——中国人

③ 德国——德国人

④ 北京——北京人

"你是哪国人"询问听话人的国籍，回答只能是"我是×国人"。例如：

"你是哪国人" is used to ask about the nationality of the listener, and the answer can only be "我是×国人". For example,

A: 你是哪国人？

B: 我是中国人。（√）

　　我是北京人。（×）

3 **我们都是欧洲人。We are both Europeans.**

"都"，副词，表示总括全部。汉语里的副词一般不能修饰名词，"都"常常出现在主语后、谓词前。例如：

"都" is an adverb which means "all". In Chinese, adverbs are usually not used to modify nouns, but used after the subject or before the predicate. For example,

S	Adv（都）	VP/Adj
你们		是经理吗？
我们	都	欢迎康爱丽。
他们（tāmen, they）		很高兴。

否定句中，"都"可放在"不"的前面，也可放在"不"的后面，但意思不同。"都不"表示全部否定，"不都"表示部分否定。例如：

In negative sentences, "都" can be used before or after "不", but the meanings are different. "都不" indicates total negation, while "不都" means partial negation. For example,

康爱丽、卡尔都是经理。	⇒他们不都是经理。
李明明是学生。	
康爱丽是法国人。	⇒他们都不是中国人。
卡尔是德国人。	

4 他也是法国人吗？ Is he French, too?

她呢？ What about her？ / 你认识她吗？ Do you know her？

汉语里，第三人称单数 tā 有两个：一个是表示男性的"他"；一个是表示女性的"她"。

In Chinese, there are two pronouns that are third person singular: one is "他", denoting male, and the other is "她", denoting female.

5 卡尔：他也是法国人吗？ 康爱丽：他不是法国人，是中国人。

Karl: Is he French, too？ Alice: No, he isn't. He is Chinese.

汉语是非疑问句和英语一般疑问句的回答形式不同。在英语里，回答一般疑问句时通常先说"yes / no"，然后再根据句首的情态动词（"am / is / are；do / does / did；can / may / will"）加以回答。汉语对于是非疑问句的回答方式多种多样：可以只回答动词，也可以回答"主语 + 动词"、"动词 + 宾语"或整个句子，但一般没必要在回答前加上类似英文中"yes / no"的"是"或"不是"。例如：

The answering pattern to the general interrogative sentence: In English, we usually answer "yes / no" first, and then complete the answer according to the modal verbs（am / is / are；do / does / did；can / may / will）at the beginning of the sentence. In Chinese, there are various ways to answer the question: The speaker can answer only with a verb, or "subject + verb", or "verb + object", or a complete sentence. But generally it is unnecessary to say "是" or "不是" first. For example,

General interrogative sentence	Answer
Is Mary a Japanese girl?	Yes, she is. / No, she isn't.
玛丽（Mǎlì, Mary）是法国女孩儿（nǚháir, girl）吗？	是。/ 不是。（V） 她是。/ 她不是。（S+V） 她是法国女孩儿。/ 她不是法国女孩儿。（Sentence）
Do you have a Chinese name?	Yes, I have. / No, I haven't.
你有中文名字吗？	有。/ 没有。（V） 有中文名字。/ 没有中文名字。（V+O） 我有中文名字。/ 我没有中文名字。（Sentence）
Do you know him?	Yes, I do. / No, I don't.
你认识他吗？	认识。/ 不认识。（V） 我认识。/ 我不认识。（S+V） 我认识他。/ 我不认识他。（Sentence）

6　那位小姐是谁？ Who is that lady?

"那"，指示代词，指示比较远的人或事物。我们在第一单元学过另一个指示代词"这"，指示比较近的人或事物。这两个是最基本的指示代词。

"那" is a demonstrative pronoun, indicating a person or thing farther away. In Unit One we have learned another demonstrative pronoun "这", which indicates a person or thing nearby. The two are the most basic demonstrative pronouns.

这两个指示代词可以单用，在句中多作主语，多用在"是"字句中。例如：

The two demonstrative pronouns may be used separately in a sentence, serving mostly as the subject in the "是"-sentence. For example,

①　这是你的中文名字吗？

②　那是我的书。

"这"、"那"的后面可以跟量词、数量词、名词，有确指的作用。例如：

"这" and "那" may be followed by a measure word, quantifier or noun, etc. They function as definite reference. For example,

③　那位小姐是李明明。

④　这三 (sān, three) 本是汉语书。

⑤　那孩子 (háizi, child) 是德国人。

注意：在口语中，单用或者后面直接加名词时，"这"说 zhè，"那"说 nà 或 nè；后面加量词或者数量词时，"这"常常说 zhèi，"那"常常说 nèi 或 nè。

Note: In oral Chinese, "这" is pronounced as zhè and "那" is pronounced as nà or nè when they are used on their own or followed by a noun; when they are followed by a measure word or quantifier, "这" is often pronounced as zhèi，and "那" is often pronounced as nèi or nè.

7 那位小姐是谁？ **Who is that lady?**

"位"，量词，用来表示人的数量，带有敬意。但是不能直接修饰"人"等词语。例如：

"位" is a measure word used to modify the number of persons, showing the speaker's courtesy and respect. But it cannot be used directly to modify the noun "人". For example,

    ① 一 (yī, a, an, one) 位人 　　　　　（ × ）
    ② 一位经理 　　　　　　　　　　　（ √ ）
    ③ 一位小姐 　　　　　　　　　　　（ √ ）
    ④ 一位法国人 　　　　　　　　　　（ √ ）

8 那位小姐是谁？ **Who is that lady?**

"谁"，疑问代词，用来问人，可以读做 shéi 和 shuí。"谁"和第一单元我们学过的疑问代词"什么"一样，都可以放在主语、宾语和定语的位置上，用法和它们在句中替代的名词的用法一样。

"谁" is an interrogative pronoun used to ask about a person. It is pronounced as shéi or shuí. Like the interrogative pronoun "什么" we learned in Unit One, "谁" can be used as a subject, an object or an attribute with the same function as the noun it replaces.

"谁"和"什么"作定语时不一样，"谁 + 的 +A"表示领属关系；"什么 +A"表示修饰关系，问事物的性质和种类。例如：

"谁" and "什么" are different when they serve as attributes. "谁 + 的 +A" indicates a possessive relationship; "什么 +A" indicates a modifying relationship to inquire about the nature or category of things. For example,

    ① A: 这是谁的书？
        B: 这是明明的书。
    ② A: 这是什么书？
        B: 这是汉语 (Hànyǔ, Chinese language) 书，不是英语 (Yīngyǔ, English) 书。

我们在第一单元学过，汉语的疑问句和陈述句的语序一样，只是把提问的部分换成不同的疑问代词。这点与英语的疑问句不同。下面我们看看疑问代词"什么、哪、谁"在句中的使用情况。

We have learned in Unit One that the word order for Chinese interrogative sentences and declarative sentences are the same, but, the parts to be asked about are replaced with different interrogave pronouns. This differs from English interrogative sentences. Now let's look at how the three interrogative pronouns "什么", "哪", "谁" are used.

陈述句 Declarative sentence	疑问句 Interrogative sentence
我叫卡尔。	你叫什么名字?
我是中国人。	您是哪国人?
那位小姐是李明明。	那位小姐是谁?
那位小姐是李明明。	哪位小姐是李明明?
我们明天见。	我们哪天见?

Jiào Wǒ Míngming ba

叫我明明吧

Please call me Mingming

Kǎ'ěr xiǎng rènshi Kāng Àilì de péngyou, Kāng Àilì wèi tāmen jièshào.

卡尔想认识康爱丽的朋友，康爱丽为他们介绍。

Karl wants to know Alice's friend and Alice is introducing them.

Kāng Àilì: Míngming, guòlai yíxià.

● 康爱丽：明明，过来一下。

Alice:　　Mingming, come here.

Lǐ Míngming zǒu guòlai.

李明明走过来。

Li Mingming comes up.

Kāng Àilì: Zhè shì wǒ de péngyou Lǐ Míngming.

○ 康爱丽：这是我的朋友李明明。

Alice:　　This is my friend, Li Mingming.

Kǎ'ěr: Lǐ xiǎojie, nǐ hǎo! Wǒ shì Kǎ'ěr, Àilì de tóngxué.

● 卡尔：李小姐，你好！我是卡尔，爱丽的同学。

Karl:　Hi, Miss Li! I'm Karl, Aili's classmate.

○ Lǐ Míngmíng: Nǐ hǎo! Jiào wǒ Míngmíng ba.
李明明： 你好！叫我明明吧。
Li Mingming: Hi, please call me Mingming.

● Kǎ'ěr: Míngmíng, nǐ shì Běijīng rén ma?
卡尔： 明明，你是北京人吗？
Karl: Mingming, are you from Beijing?

○ Lǐ Míngmíng: Wǒ bú shì Běijīng rén, wǒ shì Shànghǎi rén.
李明明： 我不是北京人，我是上海人。
Li Mingming: No, I am from Shanghai.

● Kǎ'ěr: Shànghǎi shì ge hǎo dìfang.
卡尔： 上海是个好地方。
Karl: Shanghai is a nice place.

○ Lǐ Míngmíng: Nǐ de Zhōngwén hěn hǎo.
李明明： 你的中文很好。
Li Mingming: Your Chinese is very good.

● Kǎ'ěr: Xièxie!
卡尔： 谢谢！
Karl: Thank you!

生词 Shēngcí **New Words**

1. 吧	ba	MdPt	*a particle to indicate suggestion and soften the tone of the sentence*
2. 过来	guòlai	V	to come up
3. 一下	yíxià	Q	*a quantifier used after a verb to indicate a short, quick, random or informal action*
4. 同学	tóngxué	N	classmate
5. 不	bù	Adv	no, not
6. 个	gè	M	*a common measure word*
7. 地方	dìfang	N	place, area

专有名词 Zhuānyǒu Míngcí **Proper Nouns**

1. 明明　　Míngming　　　　a Chinese student's given name
2. 李　　　Lǐ　　　　　　　a surname
3. 上海　　Shànghǎi　　　　Shanghai, one of the largest cities in China

注释 Zhùshì **Notes**

1 **明明，过来一下。Mingming, come here. ／我是卡尔，爱丽的同学。I'm Karl, Aili's classmate.**

汉语有关姓名的称谓灵活多样，可称呼对方"姓＋名"、"名"、"姓／名／姓名＋称谓词"。如人们可称"李明明"为"李明明"、"明明"、"李小姐"、"明明小姐"、"李明明小姐"。不同的称谓可以表现出人与人之间的亲疏程度。比如，亲戚、朋友、熟人、同事之间就常常只用"名"来互相称呼，如"明明"。

There are various ways to say names in Chinese, such as "surname + given name", "given name", "surname ／ given name ／ name+ title". For example, we can call "李明明" as "李明明", "明明", "李小姐", "明明小姐", and "李明明小姐". Different forms of address show different relationships between people. For example, relatives, friends, acquaintances or colleagues often call each other by their given names, like "明明".

常用的称谓词，男性有"先生"，女性有"小姐"、"女士"等。

The commonly used titles are "先生（Mr.）" for gentlemen and "小姐 (Miss)", "女士 (Ms.)" for ladies.

称呼长辈、上级、老师时，为表示礼貌和尊敬，不能直呼其名。

When addressing seniors, superiors and teachers, we cannot address them without honorific titles.

晚辈称呼长辈要使用相应的亲属称谓，如"爸爸、妈妈、爷爷、奶奶、阿姨、叔叔、姐姐、哥哥"。

The corresponding relative addresses are used for seniors, for example, "爸爸(father)", "妈妈 (mother)", "爷爷 (grandpa)", "奶奶 (grandma)", "阿姨 (aunt)", "叔叔 (uncle)", "姐姐 (elder sister)", "哥哥 (elder brother)".

下属称呼上级常用"姓＋职务"，如"王经理"。

When addressing the superiors, we often use the structure of "surname + post". For example, "王经理".

学生称呼老师或人们称呼职业为教师的人时，可以使用"姓（名）＋老师"，如"李老师"、"李阳老师"。在中国，为表示礼貌，人们常把在学校工作的人都称做"老师"，不论他是不是教师。在大学里，教授是一种职称，人们称呼教授可以使用"姓＋老师"，也可以使用"姓（名）＋职称"，如"张老师"、"张（方）教授"。

When addressing teachers, students can use "surname + 老师", like "李老师", "李阳老师". In China, in order to show courtesy, people often refer to all of the staff working at school as "老师", no matter whether they teach or not. At universities, "professor" is a title, so people address the professors by "surname + 老师" or "surname + title", like "张老师" or "张（方）教授".

2 明明，过来一下。Mingming, come here.

"V＋一下"，表示做一次或试着做。"一下"，数量词，用在动词后，也可以写做"一下儿"。例如：

"V + 一下" means to do something once or have a try. "一下" is a quantifier used after a verb. It can be changed into "一下儿" sometimes. For example,

认识一下 　　　　介绍（jièshào, to introduce）一下 　　　来一下

问一下 　　　　看（kàn, to look）一下

3 叫我明明吧。Please call me Mingming.

双宾语动词谓语句。双宾语动词谓语句是指某些谓语动词后可以带两个宾语，一般第一个宾语指人（间接宾语），第二个宾语指物（直接宾语）。间接宾语放在直接宾语的前面。这和英语里"give me a book"的语法结构类似：动词"give"后表示人的"me"是间接宾语，表示物的"a book"是直接宾语。例如：

This is a verbal predicate sentence with double objects. Some predicates can be followed by two objects; the first one denotes person (indirect object), and the second one denotes things (direct object). The indirect object precedes the direct object. This is much similar to the grammatical structure of "give me a book" in English; "me" is the indirect object following the verb "give", and "a book" is the direct object. For example,

V	O₁	O₂
叫	我	明明
告诉（gàosu, to tell）	她	我的邮箱（yóuxiāng, email address）
给（gěi, to give）	我	一本书
送（sòng, to give as a present）	卡尔	一个礼物（lǐwù, present）

注意：并不是所有的汉语动词后都可以带两个宾语。

Note: Not all Chinese verbs can be followed by two objects.

4 **叫我明明吧。** *Please call me Mingming.*

"吧"，语气助词，用在祈使句末表示建议，使语气变得较为舒缓。例如：

"吧" is a modal particle used at the end of an imperative sentence to indicate the speaker's suggestion. It can soften the tone. For example,

Sentence			MdPt（吧）
我们	去（qù, to go）		
我们	上课（shàng kè, to have a class）		
	来		
你	吃（chī, to eat）		吧。
你	问		
你	叫	我明明	

5 **上海是个好地方。** Shanghai is a nice place.

"个"，量词，用在没有专用量词的个体名词前，表示事物的单位。"个"是使用范围最广的个体量词，可以用在很多个体名词前。

"个" is a measure word used before an individual noun that has no specific measure word, indicating the unit of a thing. "个" is the most widely used measure word for nouns. It precedes many individual nouns.

汉语里，数词不能直接修饰名词，需要在数词和名词之间加入量词，构成"数词＋量词＋名词"的结构。汉语里的个体名词一般都要求搭配一个专用量词。个体量词有一百多个，常用的量词只有二三十个。例如：

In Chinese, a numeral cannot be used directly to modify a noun. A measure word is needed between the numeral and the noun, i.e. numeral + measure word + noun. Generally, nouns in Chinese collocate with their special measure words. There are over a hundred measure words in Chinese, but only 20~30 of them are commonly used. For example,

Nu	M	N
一	家（jiā, *used for enterprises*）	公司
六（liù, six）	节（jié, *used for things with subsections, joints*）	课（kè, class）

Nu	M	N
一	个	地方 学校
八（bā, eight）	名（míng, *used for people*）	学生
三	块（kuài, *used for lumps, chunks*）	面包（miànbāo, bread） 巧克力（qiǎokèlì, chocolate）
一	本	书
一	张（zhāng, *used for tables, desks, beds, etc.*）	桌子（zhuōzi, table, desk）

汉语里，有些名词（多是表示容器的）可以临时用作量词，叫借用量词。例如：

In Chinese, some nouns temporarily used as measure words are referred to as "borrowed measure words". Most of these nouns indicate the containers. For example,

Nu	M	N
一	杯（bēi, cup）	咖啡（kāfēi, coffee）
		牛奶（niúnǎi, milk）
		啤酒（píjiǔ, beer）
		饮料（yǐnliào, beverage）

在"数词 + 量词 + 名词"的结构中，当数词是"一"且这个结构不在句首时，"一"常常省略。例如：

In the structure "numeral + measure word + noun", when the numeral is "一" and this structure is not used at the beginning of the sentence, "一" is often omitted. For example,

① 上海是（一）个好地方。　　（√）

② 他是（一）个学生。　　（√）

③ 卡尔是（一）位经理。　　（√）

④ 个学生叫李明明。　　（×）

同一个名词也会因为情境的不同、数量的多少而使用不同的量词。例如：

The same noun may need different measure words based on different situations and amounts of the noun. For example,

⑤ 一个人

⑥ 一群（qún, group）人

Nǐ Zhù Zài Nǎr

你住在哪儿

Where do you live

Kāng Àilì hé Kǎ'ěr zài jiàoshì li liáotiānr.

康爱丽和卡尔在教室里聊天儿。

Alice and Karl are chatting in the classroom.

Kāng Àilì: Āi, Kǎ'ěr, nǐ zhù zài nǎr?

● 康爱丽：哎，卡尔，你住在哪儿？

Alice:　　Hey, Karl, where do you live?

Kǎ'ěr: Xuéxiào de gōngyù. Nǐ ne?

○ 卡尔：学校的公寓。你呢？

Karl:　At the school apartment. What about you?

Kāng Àilì: Wǒ zhù zài wàibian.

● 康爱丽：我住在外边。

Alice:　　I live off-campus.

生词 Shēngcí **New Words**

1. 住	zhù	V	to live, to stay, to dwell
2. 在	zài	Prep	at, in, on
3. 哪儿	nǎr	QPr	where
4. 哎	āi	MdPt	*a particle used to remind of sth.*
5. 学校	xuéxiào	N	school
6. 公寓	gōngyù	N	apartment
7. 外边	wàibian	N	outside

注释 Zhùshì **Notes**

1 你住在哪儿？**Where do you live?**

"哪儿"，疑问代词，用在特指疑问句中，询问处所，常用在口语中。和英语中的"where"类似。例如：

"哪儿"，an interrogative pronoun, is used to ask about a place. It is often used in oral Chinese, similar to "where" in English. For example,

① 你去哪儿？

② 食堂（shítáng, canteen）在哪儿？

2 你住在哪儿？**Where do you live?** / 我住在外边。**I live off-campus.**

"在"，介词。"在 + 表示处所的名词或词组"组成介词短语，放在动词后面，补充说明动作的处所，表示主语所处的位置。例如：

"在" is a preposition. The prepositional phrase "在 + noun or phrase to denote place" is put after a verb to indicate the place where the action happens, or the location of the subject. For example,

S	V	Prep（在）	Noun or phrase to denote a place（表示处所的名词或词组）
我	住	在	北京饭店（Běijīng Fàndiàn, Beijing Hotel）。
卡尔			203房间（fángjiān, room）。

"我住在外边"是"我住在学校的外边"的省略形式。当上文的语境已经给出处所所属的范围（"学校"）时，或在说话双方都知道的情况下，下文可省略。

"我住在外边" is the abbreviated form of "我住在学校的外边". When the place (school) has been given in the previous context, or known by both speakers, it can be omitted.

练习 Liànxí **Exercises**

一 跟读生词,注意发音和声调。
Read the new words after the teacher and pay attention to your pronunciation.

二 跟读课文,注意语音语调。
Read the texts after the teacher and pay attention to your pronunciation.

三 学生分组,分角色朗读课文一、二、三。
Divide the students into groups and read Texts 1, 2 & 3 in roles.

四 学生分组,不看书,分角色表演课文一、二、三。
Divide the students into groups and play the roles in Texts 1, 2 & 3 without referring to the book.

五 角色扮演。（提示：角色可以互换。）
Role play. (Note: the roles can be exchanged.)

1. 根据课文中的对话内容,用学过的词语和句子,两个学生（A 和 B）组成一组互相问答。
   Based on the dialogues in the texts, two students (A and B) work as a pair to ask and answer questions in turn with the words and sentences they have learned.

学生 A	学生 B
请问,你是哪国人?	我是……人。
……是个好地方。	谢谢。你呢?
我是……人。	你叫什么名字?
我姓……,叫……。你呢?	我叫……。
那个人是谁?	他/她是……。
你认识他/她吗?	我……。
这是我的朋友……。	认识你很高兴。
你住在哪儿?	我住在……。你呢?

2. 学习班上所有学生的国籍名称,然后由老师说出任意一个国家的名称,这个国家的学生要一一说出自己的名字、国籍,以及住在哪儿等情况。
   Learn the names of the nationalities of all the students in the class. When the teacher tells the name of a country, the student(s) from this country should tell his/her (their) name(s), nationality (ies) and where he/she (they) live(s), etc.

六 替换练习。
Substitution drills.

① 我是 德国人，你 呢？

学生	李小姐
中国人	卡尔
老师	他

② 你们 过来 一下。

来
问
见
认识

③ 叫我明明 吧。

北京见
你们过来
他们去
请进

④ 我住在 外边。

德国
法国
欧洲
北京
上海

七 用下面的词语组成句子。
Make sentences with the following words and expressions.

① 哪　人　是　您　国

② 小姐　谁　位　是　那

③ 的　老师　是　他　我　辅导

④ 我　康爱丽　同学　的　是

⑤ 地方　上海　个　是　好

⑥ 在　卡尔　哪儿　住

⑦ 公寓　他　在　学校　住　的

八 改写句子。
Rewrite the sentences.

1. Example: 我是老师，李小姐也是老师。　——→　我们都是老师。

① 卡尔是经理，李明明也是经理。　——→

② 老师欢迎我，她也欢迎我。　——→

③ 我的同学是上海人，他也是上海人。——→

2. Example: 我是学生，他是老师。　——→　我们不都是学生。

① 辅导老师过来，李明明不过来。　——→

② 老师住在学校的公寓，她住在外边。——→

3. Example: 我的同学不是欧洲人，他也不是欧洲人。

→ 他们都不是欧洲人。

① 她不叫李明明，我也不叫李明明。 →

② 我不认识他，康爱丽也不认识他。 →

九 把下面的陈述句改成一般疑问句。
Change the following declarative sentences into general interrogative sentences.

Example: 我是德国人。 → 你是德国人吗?

① 我认识他。 →

② 那位小姐是我的辅导老师。 →

③ 这是我的朋友李明明。 →

④ 叫我明明吧。 →

⑤ 上海是个好地方。 →

⑥ 我住在外边。 →

十 回答问题：两个同学一组，根据下面的问题，互相问答。回答的人请尽可能多地给出你知道的答案，如例句。下面句中 "……" 的部分请根据自己的实际情况选用。
Answer the questions: Students work in pairs to ask and answer questions in turn based on the following questions. The one who answers the questions should try to give as many answers as possible. The part of "……" in the following sentences can be replaced with your own personal information.

Example: A: 你是德国人吗?

B: 是。/不是。/我是德国人。/我不是德国人。

① 你是……吗?

② 这是你的同学吗?

③ 那是你的朋友吗?

④ 他是你的辅导老师吗?

⑤ 你的老师是北京人吗?

⑥ 北京是个好地方吗?

⑦ 你的中文好吗?

⑧ 你姓王吗?

⑨ 你叫康爱丽吗?

⑩ 你有……吗?

⑪ 你认识……吗?

⑫ 认识他你高兴吗?

⑬ 你欢迎我来北京吗?

⑭ 你住在外边吗?

 完成任务: 请用课文中学过的词语和句子完成任务。

Complete the tasks: Please complete the tasks with the words and sentences you have learned in the texts.

1. 请主动找机会与陌生人聊天,询问他/她是哪国人(哪儿人),然后向你的老师和同学介绍。
   Find a chance to chat with a stranger. Ask where he/she comes from and then introduce him/her to your teacher and classmates.

2. 你和朋友 A 约好在你的公司见面。朋友 A 来到你的办公室时,朋友 B 也在你的办公室。请你设想一下 A 和 B 的情况,并为他们介绍,或让他们互相介绍。
   You and your friend A have made an appointment to meet in your company. When A comes to your office, B, another friend of yours, is also in your office. Please introduce them to each other or ask them to introduce themselves to each other.

第三单元
UNIT 3
谈工作
Talking about one's job

你在哪儿工作
Where do you work

课文 Text	题目 Title	注释 Notes
一	汉语难吗 Is Chinese difficult to learn	1. 介词"在"(2)　The preposition "在"(2) 2. 形容词谓语句 　　The sentence with an adjectival predicate 3. "不太 +Adj" 4. 连词"可是"　The conjunction "可是" 5. 正反疑问句　The affirmative and negative question 6. 代词"每"　The pronoun "每" 7. 汉语里数字的读法 　　The pronunciation of numbers in Chinese 8. 量词"节"　The measure word "节"
二	你在哪儿工作 Where do you work	1. 量词"家"　The measure word "家" 2. 动词"当"　The verb "当" 3. 礼貌用语"抱歉"　A polite expression："抱歉" 4. 礼貌用语"没关系"　A polite expression："没关系" 5. 能愿动词"能"　The optative verb "能" 6. 带双宾语的动词"告诉" 　　The verb with double objects "告诉"
三	你最近忙吗 Are you busy recently	1. 动词"忙"　The verb "忙" 2. "V+ 什么 + 呢？" 3. "太……了" 4. "还行" 5. 时间词作状语　Time words used as adverbials 6. 介词"给"　The preposition "给" 7. 副词"真"　The adverb "真" 　　辨析："非常"、"很"、"真" 　　Discrimination："非常"，"很" and "真" 8. 语气助词"啊"　The modal particle "啊"

Hànyǔ Nán ma

汉语难吗

Is Chinese difficult to learn

Zài shítáng, Zhāng Yuǎn zuòdào Kǎ'ěr de pángbiān, tāmen liáole qǐlai.

在食堂，张远坐到卡尔的旁边，他们聊了起来。

In the canteen, Zhang Yuan is sitting beside Karl and chatting with him.

Kǎ'ěr: Nǐ hǎo!

● 卡尔：你好！

Karl:　Hello!

Zhāng Yuǎn: Nǐ hǎo! Nǐ shì liúxuéshēng ma?

○ 张远：　你好！你是留学生吗？

Zhang Yuan: Hello! Are you an international student?

Kǎ'ěr: Duì, wǒ zài Duìwài Jīngjì Màoyì Dàxué xuéxí Hànyǔ. Nǐ shì lǎoshī ma?

● 卡尔：对，我在对外经济贸易大学学习汉语。你是老师吗？

Karl:　Yes, I study Chinese at University of International Business and Economics.
　　　　Are you a teacher?

Zhāng Yuǎn: Bú shì, wǒ yě shì Jīngmào Dàxué de xuésheng. Hànyǔ nán ma?

○ 张远：　不是，我也是经贸大学的学生。汉语难吗？

Zhang Yuan: No, I am also a student of this university. Is Chinese difficult to learn?

Kǎ'ěr: Bú tài nán, kěshì Hànzì hěn nán.

● 卡尔： 不太难，可是汉字很难。

Karl:　Not too difficult, but Chinese characters are difficult.

Zhāng Yuǎn: Nǐmen de kè duō bu duō?

○ 张远： 你们的课多不多？

Zhang Yuan: Do you have many classes?

Kǎ'ěr: Hěn duō, měi tiān yǒu liù jié kè.

● 卡尔： 很多，每天有六节课。

Karl:　Yes, six classes every day.

生词　Shēngcí　New Words

1.	汉语	Hànyǔ	N	Chinese language
2.	难	nán	Adj	difficult
3.	留学生	liúxuéshēng	N	international student
4.	对	duì	Adj	yes, right, correct
5.	学习	xuéxí	V	to learn, to study
6.	学生	xuésheng	N	student
7.	太	tài	Adv	too
8.	可是	kěshì	Conj	but
9.	汉字	Hànzì	N	Chinese characters
10.	你们	nǐmen	Pr	you
11.	课	kè	N	class, lesson
12.	多	duō	Adj	many, much
13.	每	měi	Pr	every
14.	天	tiān	N	day
15.	六	liù	Nu	six
16.	节	jié	M	*a measure word*

专有名词 Zhuānyǒu Míngcí **Proper Nouns**

1. 对外经济贸易大学 Duìwài Jīngjì Màoyì Dàxué University of International Business and Economics (UIBE)

2. 经贸大学 Jīngmào Dàxué the abbreviation of UIBE

注释 Zhùshì **Notes**

1 我在对外经济贸易大学学习汉语。

I study Chinese at University of International Business and Economics.

"在"，介词，和表示处所的词语组成介宾短语，放在谓语动词前，作状语，表示动作的处所。基本结构：主语 + "在" + 处所词语 + 动词 + 宾语。例如：

The preposition "在" forms a prepositional phrase with words denoting place. The prepositional phrase is used before the predicative verb, serving as the adverbial modifier and indicating the place where the action takes place. Basic structure: Subject + "在" + place word + verb + object. For example,

S	P		V	O
	PP			
	Prep（在）	PW		
爸爸（bàba, dad）		一家电脑（diànnǎo, computer）公司	工作。	
他		一家贸易公司	当	经理。
我	在	经贸大学	学习	汉语。
你		哪儿	工作？	
你		哪儿	住？	

2 汉语难吗？Is Chinese difficult to learn?／ 汉字很难。Chinese characters are difficult.／ 你们的课多不多？Do you have many classes？

形容词谓语句。汉语中，形容词作谓语的句子称为形容词谓语句。和英语不同，汉语形容词前不能加"是"。这类句子里直接用形容词表示主语的性质或者状态等。形容词前面可以加副词作状语。例如：

In Chinese, a sentence with an adjective as the predicate is called the sentence with an adjectival predicate. It is different from English, for "是" cannot be used before the adjective in Chinese. In such a sentence, the adjective directly indicates the property or state of the subject. It is preceded by an adverb which is used as the adverbial modifier. For example,

S	P		
	Adv	Adj	Pt（吗）
他	很	好。	
我们的课	真（zhēn, really）	多。	
王经理	最近（zuìjìn, recently）	忙（máng, busy）	吗？

3 不太难。Not too difficult.

不太 +Adj。"太"，副词，用在形容词或动词前面，表示程度比一般的或者料想的高。否定形式"不太 +Adj"意思相当于"不很……"，"不太难"是"不很难"，指没有想象的难。

"不太"+Adj. "太" is an adverb used before an adjective or a verb to indicate the degree is higher than expected. The negative form "不太 +Adj" equals to "不很……"."不太难" means "不很难"; it means something is not as difficult as expected.

"难"的程度依次是：

The order of the degree of "难"：

不难 < 不太难 < 难 < 很难 < 太难（了）

4 可是汉字很难。But Chinese characters are difficult.

"可是"，连词，表示转折，用在句子或者段落中，表示后边的分句不是顺着前一分句的意思说下去，而是发生转折，变成了相反或者相对的意思。例如：

"可是" is a conjunction which indicates transition. It is used in a sentence or a paragraph to indicate the latter clause doesn't follow the meaning of the preceding one, but shifts to an opposite meaning. For example,

Clause 1	Conj（可是）	Clause 2
汉语不难，		汉字很难。
他不是中国人，	可是	每天说汉语。
汉字不多，		很难。

5 你们的课多不多？ Do you have many classes？

正反疑问句。这是汉语中另一种表示疑问的句式，是同时把肯定形式和否定形式都提出来，让听话人选择其中的一种，句末不再用"吗"。谓语可以是形容词，也可以是动词。比较下面的一般疑问句和正反疑问句：

The affirmative and negative question is another form of questions in Chinese. The speaker puts forward both the affirmative and negative forms for listeners to choose. "吗" is no longer used at the end of the sentence. The predicate is an adjective or a verb. Compare the following general interrogative sentences and affirmative and negative questions.

一般疑问句 General interrogative sentences	正反疑问句 Affirmative and negative questions
汉语难吗？	汉语难不难？
老师好吗？	老师好不好？
天气（tiānqì, weather）热（rè, hot）吗？	天气热不热？
她是你的朋友吗？	她是不是你的朋友？
我们去经贸大学，你去吗？	我们去经贸大学，你去不去？
他学汉语，你学吗？	他学汉语，你学不学？

6 每天有六节课。Six classes every day.

"每"，代词，表示全部中的任何一个。用在量词或名词前，意思是所有的都怎么样。常在谓语动词前加上"都"，和"每"呼应，强调没有例外，全都这样，说明主语位置上的时间是周遍性的。例如：

"每" is a pronoun which indicates any one in a whole. It is used before a measure word or a noun, describing the state of every one in a whole. "都" is often added before the predicate to correspond with "每……" before it to stress that there is no exception and to show that the time word used as the subject of the sentence denotes sth. happens on a regular basis. For example,

S	P		
	Adv	V/Adj	O
每天	（都）	有	六节课。
每天上午（shàngwǔ, morning）	（都）	有	汉语课。
每天早上（zǎoshang, morning）	（都）	跑步（pǎo bù, to run）。	
每天晚上（wǎnshang, night, evening）	（都）	发（fā, to send）	邮件（yóujiàn, email）。
每天	（都很）	忙。	

7 每天有六节课。**Six classes every day.**

"六"，数词，可以作为数字，也可以用来表示号码或者数量。

"六" is a numeral. It is used as a figure as well as a number or an amount.

汉语里数字的读法：

The pronunciation of numbers in Chinese:

1	2	3	4	5	6	7	8	9	10
一	二	三	四	五	六	七	八	九	十
yī	èr	sān	sì	wǔ	liù	qī	bā	jiǔ	shí

11	12	13	14	15
十一	十二	十三	十四	十五
shíyī	shí'èr	shísān	shísì	shíwǔ

21	22	26	27	28
二十一	二十二	二十六	二十七	二十八
èrshíyī	èrshí'èr	èrshíliù	èrshíqī	èrshíbā

31	32	39	40	99
三十一	三十二	三十九	四十	九十九
sānshíyī	sānshí'èr	sānshíjiǔ	sìshí	jiǔshíjiǔ

100	102	122	250	252
一百	一百零二	一百二十二	二百五（十）	二百五十二
yìbǎi	yìbǎi líng èr	yìbǎi èrshí'èr	èrbǎi wǔ (shí)	èrbǎi wǔshí'èr

1000	1002	3010	4015	6800
一千	一千零二	三千零一十	四千零一十五	六千八（百）
yìqiān	yìqiān líng èr	sānqiān líng yīshí	sìqiān líng yīshíwǔ	liùqiān bā (bǎi)

7920	6792	10,000	21,000
七千九百二（十）	六千七百九十二	一万	两万一（千）
qīqiān jiǔbǎi èr (shí)	liùqiān qībǎi jiǔshí'èr	yíwàn	liǎngwàn yì (qiān)

8 每天有六节课。**Six classes every day.**

"节"，量词，用于分段的事物或文章前面，表示该事物或文章的数量。例如：

"节" is a measure word. It is used before a thing or an article which is divided into sections to indicate the quantity of the thing or article. For example,

语法（yǔfǎ, grammar）课	8:00~8:45	一节课	
口语（kǒuyǔ, spoken language）课	9:00~9:45	一节课	三节课
听力（tīnglì, listening）课	10:00~10:45	一节课	
语法、口语、听力——三门（mén, *a measure word for classes*）课			

Nǐ Zài Nǎr Gōngzuò

你在哪儿工作

Where do you work

Jiàoshì li, Kāng Àilì hé Kǎ'ěr zài liáotiānr.

教室里，康爱丽和卡尔在聊天儿。

Alice and Karl are chatting in the classroom.

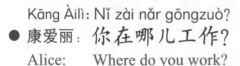

Kāng Àilì: Nǐ zài nǎr gōngzuò?

● 康爱丽：你在哪儿工作？

Alice:　　Where do you work?

Kǎ'ěr: Wǒ zài yì jiā diànnǎo gōngsī gōngzuò. Nǐ ne?

○ 卡尔：我在一家电脑公司工作。你呢？

Karl:　　I work at a computer company. And you?

Kāng Àilì: Wǒ zài yì jiā màoyì gōngsī dāng jīnglǐ. Zhè shì wǒ de míngpiàn.

● 康爱丽：我在一家贸易公司当经理。这是我的名片。

Alice:　　I am a manager at a trading company. This is my business card.

Kǎ'ěr: Bàoqiàn, wǒ méiyǒu míngpiàn.

○ 卡尔：抱歉，我没有名片。

Karl:　　Sorry, I do not have a business card.

Kāng Àilì: Méi guānxi. Nǐ néng gàosu wǒ nǐ de yóuxiāng ma?

● 康爱丽： 没关系。你能告诉我你的邮箱吗？

　　Alice:　　It doesn't matter. Can you tell me your email address?

Kǎ'ěr: Hǎo de. Wǒ de yóuxiāng shì Karl@hotmail.com.

○ 卡尔： 好的。我的邮箱是Karl@hotmail.com。

　　Karl:　　OK! My email address is Karl@hotmail.com.

	生词 Shēngcí	**New Words**		
1.	工作	gōngzuò	V/N	to work; job
2.	一	yī	Nu	a, an, one
3.	家	jiā	M	*a measure word*
4.	电脑	diànnǎo	N	computer
5.	公司	gōngsī	N	company
6.	贸易	màoyì	N	trade
7.	当	dāng	V	to serve as
8.	名片	míngpiàn	N	business card
9.	抱歉	bàoqiàn	Adj	sorry
10.	没有	méiyǒu	V	not
11.	没关系	méi guānxi	IE	It doesn't matter.
12.	能	néng	OpV	can
13.	告诉	gàosu	V	to tell
14.	邮箱	yóuxiāng	N	mailbox, email address

注释 Zhùshì **Notes**

1 我在一家电脑公司工作。**I work at a computer company.**

"家"，量词，可以用在"公司、学校、银行、邮局、饭店"等名词前。例如：

"家" is a measure word used before nouns like "公司", "学校", "银行", "邮局", "饭店", etc. For example,

Nu	M（家）	N
一		公司
八		学校
三	家	银行（yínháng, bank）
四		邮局（yóujú, post office）
五		饭店（fàndiàn, restaurant）

2 我在一家贸易公司当经理。**I am a manager at a trading company.**

"当"，动词，意思是"担任、充当"，可以和表示职业、职位或者职称的词语连用，表示担任什么工作或者职务。例如：

"当" is a verb which means "to work as". It is used together with a word denoting occupation, position or title, indicating his or her job or position. For example,

① 他在公司当经理。

② 她在小学（xiǎoxué, primary school）当老师。

③ 我在大学当领导（lǐngdǎo, leader）。

3 抱歉。**Sorry.**

"抱歉"，礼貌用语，一般用在正式场合，表示道歉或遗憾。口语中也常用"对不起"。

"抱歉" is a polite expression generally used in formal occasions to show somebody's apology or regret. "对不起" is often used in oral Chinese.

4 没关系。It doesn't matter.

"没关系"，礼貌用语，常用来回答"对不起"。

"没关系" is a polite expression often used in response to "对不起".

5 你能告诉我你的邮箱吗？Can you tell me your email address?

"能"，能愿动词，用在动词前。这里表示情理上的许可，多用在疑问句和否定句中。例如：

"能" is an optative verb used before a verb. It indicates permission often used in interrogative and negative sentences. For example,

① 我太忙，不能去。

② 这是教室，不能抽烟（chōu yān, to smoke）！

"能……吗" 表示询问、请求。例如：

"能……吗" is used to indicate inquiry or request. For example,

S	OpV（能）	V/ VP	Pt（吗）
你		告诉我你的邮箱	
你	能	去上海	吗？
我们		进来	

6 你能告诉我你的邮箱吗？Can you tell me your email address?

"告诉"，动词，可以带双宾语。基本结构："告诉 + sb. + sth."。例如：

"告诉" is a verb which can be followed by two objects. The basic structure is "告诉 + sb.+ sth.". For example,

V（告诉）	O₁（sb.）	O₂（sth.）
	他。	
请告诉	我	你的邮箱。
	我	你的老师是谁。

Nǐ Zuìjìn Máng ma

你最近忙吗

Are you busy recently

Zài lùshang, Kāng Àilì hé Kǎ'ěr biān zǒu biān liáotiānr.

在路上，康爱丽和卡尔边走边聊天儿。

Alice and Karl are chatting while walking.

Kāng Àilì: Nǐ zuìjìn máng ma?

● 康爱丽：你最近忙吗?

Alice:　　Are you busy recently?

Kǎ'ěr: Fēicháng máng.

○ 卡尔：非常忙。

Karl:　　Yes, very busy.

Kāng Àilì: Máng shénme ne?

● 康爱丽：忙什么呢?

Alice:　　What are you up to?

Kǎ'ěr: Zuìjìn gōngsī de shìr tài duō le.

○ 卡尔：最近公司的事儿太多了。

Karl:　　There are so many things at the company recently.

Kāng Àilì: Nǐmen gōngsī de shēngyi hěn hǎo ba?

● 康爱丽：你们公司的生意很好吧？

Alice: How is the business in your company?

Kǎ'ěr: Hái xíng, zuìjìn shìchǎng hěn hǎo, yǒu hěn duō xīn kèhù.

○ 卡尔：还行，最近市场很好，有很多新客户。

Karl: It is OK. The market is good, and there are many new clients.

Kāng Àilì: Nǐ shàngwǎng ma?

● 康爱丽：你上网吗？

Alice: Do you surf the Internet?

Kǎ'ěr: Dāngrán, wǒ měi tiān wǎnshang dōu gěi wǒ de tóngshì fā yóujiàn.

○ 卡尔：当然，我每天晚上都给我的同事发邮件。

Karl: Of course, I send emails to my colleagues every night.

Kāng Àilì: Nǐ zhēn máng a!

● 康爱丽：你真忙啊！

Alice: How busy you are!

生词　Shēngcí　New Words

1. 最近	zuìjìn	Adv	recently, lately
2. 忙	máng	Adj / V	busy; to be busy
3. 非常	fēicháng	Adv	very much
4. 事（儿）	shì (r)	N	thing(s), affair(s)
5. 了	le	Pt	*a particle*
6. 生意	shēngyi	N	business
7. 还	hái	Adv	passably, fairly
8. 行	xíng	V	OK
9. 市场	shìchǎng	N	market
10. 新	xīn	Adj	new
11. 客户	kèhù	N	client
12. 上网	shàng wǎng	V//O	to surf the Internet
13. 当然	dāngrán	Adv	of course, certainly

14. 晚上	wǎnshang	N	night, evening
15. 给	gěi	V/Prep	to give; to, for
16. 同事	tóngshì	N	colleague
17. 发	fā	V	to send
18. 邮件	yóujiàn	N	email
19. 真	zhēn	Adv	really
20. 啊	a	MdPt	*a particle used to strengthen the tone*

注释 Zhùshì **Notes**

1 忙什么呢? **What are you up to?**

"忙",这里是动词,表示急迫不停地、加紧地做。"忙什么呢",在口语中用来问别人在做什么或为什么忙,回答时说明做什么就可以了,如"发邮件、写作业"等。本句中省略了主语"你"。

"忙" is a verb here. It indicates doing something hurriedly and continuously. "忙什么呢" is often used in oral Chinese to ask people what they are doing or why they are so busy. As an answer, we only need to say things we are doing, such as "发邮件","写作业", etc. The subject "你" is omitted in this sentence.

2 忙什么呢? **What are you up to?**

"V+什么+呢",可以用来询问动作正在进行的内容。注意:特指问句的句末不能用"吗",可以用"呢",表示疑问的语气。例如:

"V+什么+呢" can be used to ask what is going on. It is noteworthy that "吗" cannot be used at the end of a special interrogative sentence, "呢" may be used instead to indicate an interrogative tone. For example,

S	V	QPr (什么)	MdPt (呢)
(王老师)	看		
(你)	吃		
(她)	做 (zuò, to do)	什么	呢?
(卡尔)	笑 (xiào, to laugh)		

3 最近公司的事儿太多了。There are so many things at the company recently.

"太……了"，表示程度很高，也可以用在赞叹中。例如：

"太……了" denotes a high degree. It is also used for compliment. For example,

    ① 今天太热了！

    ② 我太忙了！

    ③ 作业（zuòyè, homework）太多了！

    ④ 你的汉语太好了！

4 还行。It's OK.

"还行"，口语常用语，意思是"一般"。

This is an oral Chinese expression, meaning "just so so".

"还"，副词，程度上表示勉强过得去（一般是往好的方面说）。例如：

"还" is an adverb, indicating "just passable" (usually from a positive perspective). For example,

    ① 我的英语还不错。

"行"，动词，表示可以。汉语里，"还行"常用来回答别人的询问或称赞，是回避实际情况或是比较谦虚的说法。例如：

"行" is a verb indicating "OK". In Chinese, "还行" is often used in respond to other's inquiry or compliment. It is either to avoid mentioning the real situation or to show modesty. For example,

    ② A: 你的汉语很好！

        B: 还行。

5 我每天晚上都给我的同事发邮件。I send emails to my colleagues every night.

"每天晚上"，时间词作状语。表示时间的词语如"三点、八点半、明天、今天"等常常出现在谓语动词或形容词前作状语。例如：

"每天晚上" is a time adverbial. The words denoting time, such as "三点"，"八点半"，"明天"，"今天" can be used as adverbials before verbal predicates or adjectives. For example,

S	P	
	TW	VP/Adj
我	每天6:15	起床（qǐ chuáng, to get up）。
他	3:00	回家（huí jiā, to go home）。
我们	8:30	上课。
他们	明天	休息（xiūxi, to have a rest）。
他	今天（jīntiān, today）	很忙。
他	每天	都给他的女朋友（nǚpéngyou, girlfriend）买（mǎi, to buy）花（huā, flower）。

6 　**我每天晚上都给我的同事发邮件。I send emails to my colleagues every night.**

"给"，介词，用来引进动作的对象，和后面的宾语组成介宾短语，放在谓语动词前。基本结构：给 +sb. +VP。例如：

"给" is a preposition used to introduce the receiver of the action. It forms a prepositional phrase with the following object and is placed before the verb. The basic structure is "给 +sb.+VP". For example,

S	P	
	Prep（给）+sb.	VP
我	给你	发邮件。
卡尔	给他的妈妈（māma, mum）	打电话（dǎ diànhuà, to call）。
我	给我的朋友	写信（xiě xìn, to write a letter）。

7 　**你真忙啊！How busy you are！**

"真"，副词，"实在、的确"的意思。用在形容词、动词前，表示强调，有时句末可以用表示语气的助词"啊"。例如：

"真" is an adverb which means "really, exactly". It is used before an adjective or a verb to denote emphasis. Sometimes the modal particle "啊" is put at the end of the sentence. For example,

S	P	
	Adv（真）	Adj / VP
汉语		难（啊）！
公司的生意		好！
天气	真	热！
汉字		难写（xiě, to write）（啊）！
他		是一位好老师！

辨析 Discrimination：　"非常"、"很"、"真"

这三个词都是副词，都可以放在形容词的前面，表示程度相当高，有时可以替换使用。但是"非常"的意思比较强烈；"很"的程度要根据具体意思来判断；"真"强调"确实是这样"。

All these three words are adverbs and can be put before adjectives to denote a high degree. They can be used alternatively sometimes. The meaning of "非常" is very strong, the degree of "很" needs to be judged according to the actual situation; "真" means "indeed" or "really".

8 你真忙啊！How busy you are!

"啊"，语气助词，用在感叹句末尾，表示增强语气。读轻声。例如：

"啊", a modal particle spoken in the neutral tone, is used at the end of an exclamatory sentence to reinforce the tone. For example,

① 你们的课真多啊！

② 风景（fēngjǐng, scenery）真美（měi, beautiful）啊！

③ 你的中文真好啊！

一 跟读生词,注意发音和声调。
Read the new words after the teacher and pay attention to your pronunciation.

二 跟读课文,注意语音语调。
Read the texts after the teacher and pay attention to your pronunciation.

三 学生分组，分角色朗读课文一、二、三。
Divide the students into groups and read Texts 1, 2 & 3 in roles.

四 学生分组，不看书，分角色表演课文一、二、三。
Divide the students into groups and play the roles in Texts 1, 2 & 3 without referring to the book.

五 角色扮演。(提示：角色可以互换。)
Role play. (Note: the roles can be exchanged.)

1. 根据课文一学过的内容完成一段对话：两人一组，模仿第一次见面的情景，一个人主动和另一人谈话，寻找话题（如关于学习或工作的），然后双方互问互答。
Complete a dialogue based on what you've learned in the texts: Students work in pairs to imitate the scene when they first meet. One initiates the conversation and picks up a topic (on study or work) and then the two ask and answer questions in turn.

2. 两个学生组成一组，根据课文中的对话内容，运用学过的词语和句子互相问答。
Students work in pairs to ask and answer questions in turn with the words and sentences they have learned based on the dialogues in the texts.

学生 A	学生 B
你在哪儿工作?	我……工作。
你最近忙吗?	我……。
你能告诉我你的邮箱吗?	当然，我的邮箱是……。
你给你的同事发邮件吗?	（肯定　Affirmative）……。 （否定　Negative）……。

六 替换练习。
Substitution drills.

① 你　在哪儿　工作?

她	经贸大学	学习汉语
我	公司	给同事发邮件
客户	美国（Měiguó, USA）	给我打电话
王老师	这儿（zhèr, here）	上课

② 汉字　很难。

汉语	不难
我们的课	很多
她的同事	非常忙
他们公司的客户	不太多

③ 课不多，可是　很难。

客户不太多	我们每天都有新的客户
汉字很少	很难
经理不在这儿	她每天给我们发邮件
他不是中国人	汉语非常好

④ 你们的课　多不　多?

汉语	难
经贸大学的学生	忙
你的同事	多
他的生意	好

⑤ 你　能　告诉我你的邮箱　吗?

我	不写汉字
你	给我的同事发邮件
我们	在这儿聊天儿（liáo tiānr, to chat）
我	在这儿工作

⑥ 我　告诉　你　我的邮箱。

老师	我们	汉字不难
经理	她	生意很好
我们	你	我们的名字
他	我	他很忙

⑦ 你　最近　忙　吗?

你的同事	好
公司的客户	多
经理	高兴
公司的生意	好

⑧ 我　每天晚上　都　给　我的同事　发邮件。

我	每天早上	妈妈	打电话
他	每天	客户	发邮件
卡尔	每月（yuè, month）	他的朋友	写信
经理	每周（zhōu, week）	他们	开会（kāi huì, to have a meeting）

⑨ 你 真 忙啊!

你的中文名字	好听 （hǎotīng, sounds good）
我们的课	多
经理	好
这本书	新

七 用下面的词语组成句子。

Make sentences with the following words and expressions.

① 吗 你 留学生 是

② 是 经贸大学 我 的 也 学生

③ 六 每天 有 课 节

④ 吗 汉语 难

⑤ 当 我 经理 贸易公司 一家 在

⑥ 名片 我 这 是 的

⑦ 呢 什么 忙

⑧ 事儿 最近 多 太 公司 了 的

⑨ 公司 你们 很 的 好 生意 吧

八 用 "呢"、"吗"、"吧"、"啊" 填空。
Fill in the blanks with "呢", "吗", "吧" or "啊".

① 你的课多 （   ）？

② 汉字难不难 （   ）？

③ 你在哪儿工作 （   ）？

④ 她真是个大忙人（dàmángrén，a busy person）（   ）！

⑤ 你最近忙什么 （   ）？

⑥ 你的汉语很好 （   ）！

九 给 "哪儿" 选择一个合适的位置。
Choose the right places for "哪儿".

① 你 A 在 B 学习 C 汉语？　　（   ）

② 你的 A 公司 B 在 C 呢？　　（   ）

③ 你的 A 客户 B 在 C？　　（   ）

④ 你们 A 是 B 的 C 学生？　　（   ）

⑤ A 有 B 名片 C？　　（   ）

⑥ 你的 A 经理 B 在 C？　　（   ）

十 完成任务：请用课文中学过的词语和句子完成任务。

Complete the tasks: Please complete the tasks with the words and sentences you have learned in the texts.

1. 采访一位中国朋友，问他在哪儿工作、公司在哪儿、邮箱是什么等情况，并记录下来。

   Interview a Chinese friend. Ask the name and location of the company he works for and his email address, and then write it down.

2. 在课堂上，将之前采访到的情况向老师和同学进行介绍。

   Make a presentation in class about the information you have got from the interview.

第四单元 UNIT 4
时间的表达
Expressions of time

现在几点
What time is it

课文 Text	题目 Title	注释 Notes
一	现在几点 What time is it	1. 疑问代词"几" The interrogative pronoun "几" 2. 副词"没" The adverb "没" 3. "您（你）知道……吗？" 4. 钟点表示法 Expressions of hours and minutes 5. 辨析："两"和"二" Discrimination:"两" and "二" 6. "（你）准备好了吗？" 7. 辨析："我们"和"咱们" 　　Discrimination:"我们" and "咱们" 8. 副词"别" The adverb "别" 9. 时间表达法 Expressions of time
二	你每天几点 起床 What time do you get up every day	1. 方位词"以后" The locality noun "以后" 2. "先……，然后……" 3. 方位词"左右" The locality noun "左右" 4. "来得及"／"来不及" 5. 连词"所以" The conjunction "所以" 6. 副词"有时候" The adverb "有时候" 7. "没办法！"
三	卡尔的一天 One day of Karl's	1. 方位词"以前" The locality noun "以前" 2. "从……到……" 3.（1）"星期"的表示法 　　　Expressions of the days of a week 　（2）"年"的表示法 Expressions of the year 　（3）"月"的表示法 Expressions of the month 　（4）"日"的表示法 Expressions of the date 　（5）年、月、日、星期的顺序 The order of the 　　　week, month, date and year

Xiànzài Jǐ Diǎn

现在几点

What time is it

Kāng Àilì hé Kǎ'ěr yào qù kāihuì.

康爱丽和卡尔要去开会。

Alice and Karl are going to a meeting.

Kāng Àilì: Kǎ'ěr, xiànzài jǐ diǎn?

● 康爱丽: 卡尔，现在几点？

Alice:　　Karl, what time is it?

Kǎ'ěr: Wǒ méi dài biǎo, bù zhīdào. Wáng lǎoshī, nín zhīdao xiànzài jǐ diǎn ma?

○ 卡尔: 我没戴表，不知道。王老师，您知道现在几点吗？

Karl:　　I don't know. I have't worn my watch. Do you know what time it is, Mr. Wang?

Wáng lǎoshī: Chà liǎng fēn yī diǎn.

● 王老师: 差两分一点。

Mr. Wang:　　Two minutes to one.

Kāng Àilì: Kǎ'ěr, jīntiān xiàwǔ de Zhōngguó jīngjì yántǎohuì jǐ diǎn kāishǐ?

○ 康爱丽: 卡尔，今天下午的中国经济研讨会几点开始？

Alice:　　Karl, what time will the Seminar on Chinese Economy start this afternoon?

Kǎ'ěr: Yī diǎn bàn kāishǐ, nǐ zhǔnbèi hǎo le ma?
● 卡尔：一点半开始，你准备好了吗？
Karl: Half past one. Are you ready?

Kāng Àilì: Zhǔnbèi hǎo le, zánmen zǒu ba!
○ 康爱丽：准备好了，咱们走吧！
Alice: Yes, let's go.

Wáng lǎoshī: Nǐmen kuài qù ba! Bié chídào!
● 王老师：你们快去吧！别迟到！
Mr. Wang: Hurry up! Don't be late.

Kāng Àilì: Hǎo de, Wáng lǎoshī, míngtiān jiàn!
○ 康爱丽：好的，王老师，明天见！
Alice: OK, see you tomorrow, Mr. Wang.

Kǎ'ěr: Zàijiàn, Wáng lǎoshī.
● 卡尔：再见，王老师。
Karl: Goodbye, Mr. Wang.

生词　Shēngcí　**New Words**

1.	现在	xiànzài	N	now
2.	几	jǐ	Nu	how many
3.	点	diǎn	M	o'clock
4.	没	méi	Adv	not
5.	戴	dài	V	to wear
6.	表	biǎo	N	watch
7.	知道	zhīdào	V	to know
8.	差	chà	V	to (*indicating that there is a certain amount of time before a particular time*)
9.	两	liǎng	Nu	two
10.	分	fēn	M	minute
11.	今天	jīntiān	N	today
12.	下午	xiàwǔ	N	afternoon
13.	经济	jīngjì	N	economy

14. 研讨会	yántǎohuì	N	seminar
15. 开始	kāishǐ	V	to begin, to start
16. 半	bàn	Nu	half
17. 准备	zhǔnbèi	V	to prepare
18. 咱们	zánmen	Pr	we, us
19. 走	zǒu	V	to walk
20. 快	kuài	Adj	fast
21. 去	qù	V	to go
22. 别	bié	Adv	don't
23. 迟到	chídào	V	to be late
24. 明天	míngtiān	N	tomorrow

注释　Zhùshì　Notes

1　现在几点？What time is it?

"几"，用在特指问句中作疑问代词，用来询问数量。当问话人觉得数目不太大、可能不超过 10 时，常用 "几" 提问。"几" 应放在量词和名词前，即 "几＋量词＋名词"。例如：

"几" is used to ask about the amount in special questions. When the questioner thinks that the amount may not exceed 10, "几" is often used, i.e., "几 + measure word + noun". "几" is used before the measure word and the noun. For example,

① 您几位？

② 一星期（xīngqī, week）有几天？

③ 你们班有几个（名）学生？

④ 你们公司有几名员工（yuángōng, staff）？

⑤ 你们家（jiā, family, home）有几口（kǒu, *a measure word for people*）人？

⑥ 这是几本书？

注意：询问时间时常用 "几点"，如 "你们几点上课"；询问具体日期时常用 "几号"，如 "今天几号"。

Note: "几点" is often used to ask about the time, for example, "你们几点上课"; "几号" is used to ask about the date, for example, "今天几号".

2 **我没戴表。I haven't worn my watch.**

"没", 副词, 用在动词前, 表示否定, 意思是不存在或没发生过。 例如:

"没" is an adverb used before a verb to indicate negation. It means something did not exist or happen. For example,

S	P		
	Adv（没）	V	O
我	没	发	邮件。
他		去	中国。

辨析 Discrimination: "没"、"不"

（1） "没" 和 "不" 都可以用在动词前表示否定, "没" 限于指过去和现在, 不能用于将来; "不" 可以指过去、现在或将来。例如:

Both "没" and "不" can be used before verbs to denote negation. The word "没" only negates the past and the present, but not the future, while the word "不" negates the past, the present, and the future. For example,

① 他昨天没来学校。

② 他今天没上课。

③ 昨天不上课, 今天不上课, 明天也不上课, 休息三天。

（2）"没" 可以用来表示客观的叙述, 否定动作或者变化已经发生; "不" 用来表示主观愿望, 否定某种意愿或者事物有某种性质和状态。例如:

"没" is used for objective narration, negating an action or a change that has happened. "不" denotes a subjective will, negating a wish or desire, or the property or state of something. For example,

④ 他没买。（"买" 的这种行为没有发生, 是已经客观存在的情况 The action of "买" does not happen, which is the objective situation.）

⑤ 他不买。（他主观上不愿意买 He doesn't want to buy.）

3 **您知道现在几点吗？Do you know what time it is?**

"您（你）知道……吗" 表示想知道别人对事实或道理是否有认识、了解。这和英语里的 "Do you know …" 相似。这是一个是非疑问句, 肯定的回答是 "知道", 否定的回答是 "不知道"。动词 "知道" 后的宾语可以是词, 也可以是句子。例如:

"您（你）知道……吗" indicates that the questioner wants to know whether the listener knows or understands something. It is similar to "Do you know..." in English. The affirmative answer is "知道" and the negative answer is "不知道". The verb "知道" may be followed by a phrase or a sentence. For example,

你知道	N/clause	Pt（吗）
你知道	经贸大学	吗？
	康爱丽	
	现在几点	
	他是哪国人	
	他是谁	
	谁是王老师	

4 差两分一点。 Two minutes to one.

钟点表示法：

Expressions of hours and minutes：

（1）汉语里用"……点……分"表示钟点。在口语中，当"分"前是两位数时，"分"可以省略。

"……点……分" is often used in Chinese to denote time. When the number before "分" is a double-digit number, "分" is omitted.

（2）"分"前是一位数时，要在数字和"分"前加"零"或"过"。

When the number before "分" is of one-digit, "零" or "过" is often added before the number and "分".

（3）"十五分"可以说成"一刻"。

Fifteen minutes is "一刻 (a quarter)".

（4）"三十分"可以说成"半"。

Thirty minutes is "半 (half)".

（5）接近下一个钟点时，可以说"……点差……分"或者"差……分……点"。

When the time is close to the next hour, it is "……点差……分" or "差……分……点".

	Expression 1	Expression 2	Expression 3	Expression 4
2:20	两点二十分 liǎng diǎn èrshí fēn	两点二十 liǎng diǎn èrshí		
3:54	三点五十四分 sān diǎn wǔshísì fēn	三点五十四 sān diǎn wǔshísì	四点差六分 sì diǎn chà liù fēn	差六分四点 chà liù fēn sì diǎn
1:05	一点零五分 yī diǎn líng wǔ fēn	一点过五分 yī diǎn guò wǔ fēn	一点零五 yī diǎn líng wǔ	
5:15	五点十五分 wǔ diǎn shíwǔ fēn	五点一刻 wǔ diǎn yí kè	五点十五 wǔ diǎn shíwǔ	
7:45	七点四十五（分） qī diǎn sìshíwǔ（fēn）	七点三刻 qī diǎn sān kè	八点差一刻 bā diǎn chà yí kè	差一刻八点 chà yí kè bā diǎn
6:30	六点三十分 liù diǎn sānshí fēn	六点半 liù diǎn bàn	六点三十 liù diǎn sānshí	
8:10	八点十分 bā diǎn shí fēn			

5 差两分一点。**Two minutes to one.**

汉语里，"2" 可用 "二" 表示，也可用 "两" 表示。

In Chinese, "2" is indicated by "二" or "两".

辨析 Discrimination: "两"、"二"

（1）在普通话里，作为数字，"二" 可单用，"两" 不行。如 "1、2、3" 读成 "一、二、三"，不读 "一、两、三"。

In Mandarin Chinese, "二" as a figure can be used on its own, but "两" cannot. For example, "1、2、3" is pronounced as "一、二、三", not "一、两、三".

（2）如果 "2" 后有量词，常读做 "两"。"2" 在一些度量词如 "米、吨、公里" 等前也常读做 "两"。例如：

"2" is often pronounced as "两" if followed by a measure word. It is also pronounced this way if preceded by words like "米"，"吨" or "公里". For example,

① 两个人　　　liǎng ge rén　　　two people

② 两本书　　　liǎng běn shū　　　two books

③ 两斤 / 二斤　liǎng jīn/èr jīn　　two *jin* (one kilogram)

④ 两吨　　　　liǎng dūn　　　two tons

| ⑤ | 两米 | liǎng mǐ | two meters |
| ⑥ | 两公里 | liǎng gōnglǐ | two kilometers |

（3）当"2"作为多位数中的个位数时，不管是不是在量词前，都读做"二"。例如：

When "2" is a single digit in a multi-digit number, it is pronounced as "二" no matter whether it is before a measure word. For example,

⑦	22	二十二	èrshí'èr	twenty-two
⑧	42	四十二	sìshí'èr	forty-two
⑨	￥22	二十二块钱	èrshí'èr kuài qián	twenty-two *kuai*

（4）在序数、小数、分数等中，"2"都读做"二"。例如：

"2" is pronounced as "二" in ordinal numbers, decimal numbers and fractions. For example,

第+2	第二	dì èr	the second
0.22	零点二二	líng diǎn èr èr	zero point two two
2/5	五分之二	wǔ fēnzhī èr	two fifths
2%	百分之二	bǎi fēnzhī èr	two percent

6 你准备好了吗？Are you ready?

"准备好了吗"，用来询问别人准备的情况，可单独使用，与英语的"Are you ready"相似；也可在前面加主语，主语可以是完成动作的人，也可以是需要完成的事儿。例如：

"准备好了吗" is used to ask whether the other party is ready. It can be used on its own, which is similar to "Are you ready" in English. It can also be preceded by a subject, and the subject can be the person to finish the action or the thing to be finished. For example,

S	P
你们	
研讨会	准备好了吗？
问题	

肯定回答 The affirmative answer	准备好了。/ 好了。
否定回答 The negative answer	没准备好。/ 没有。

7 咱们走吧！ **Let's go.**

辨析 Discrimination： "我们"、"咱们"

用"咱们"，表示包括说话人和听话人；用"我们"，有时候可以不包括听话人。例如：

"咱们" is used to include both the speaker and the listener, while sometimes when "我们" is used, the listener is not included. For example,

> 康爱丽、卡尔是同学，王老师是他们的老师。李明明不是康爱丽、卡尔的同学，王老师不是她的老师。
>
> 康爱丽和卡尔说话时可以说：
>
> When Alice talks to Karl, she can say:
>
> 王老师是咱们老师。
>
> 康爱丽、卡尔和李明明说话时应该说：
>
> When Alice and Karl talk to Li Mingming, they can say:
>
> 王老师是我们老师。

8 别迟到！ **Don't be late！**

"别"，副词，后面可加动词或动词词组，表示禁止或劝阻别人做某事。例如：

"别", an adverb, can be followed by a verb or a verbal phrase to forbid others to do something or to stop others doing something. For example,

Adv（别）	V / VP
别	迟到！
	去那儿！
	走！
	说话！ （shuō huà，to speak）

9 明天见！ **See you tomorrow．**

时间表达法：

Expressions of time:

June 29	前天	qiántiān	the day before yesterday
June 30	昨天	zuótiān	yesterday
July 1	今天	jīntiān	today
July 2	明天	míngtiān	tomorrow
July 3	后天	hòutiān	the day after tomorrow

Nǐ Měi Tiān Jǐ Diǎn Qǐchuáng

你每天几点起床

What time do you get up every day

Kǎ'ěr hé Kāng Àilì zài jiàoshì li liáotiānr.

卡尔和康爱丽在教室里聊天儿。

Karl and Alice are chatting in the classroom.

Kǎ'ěr: Nǐ měi tiān jǐ diǎn qǐchuáng?

● 卡尔: 你每天几点起床？

Karl: What time do you get up every day?

Kāng Àilì: Wǒ měi tiān liù diǎn yí kè qǐchuáng, qǐchuáng yǐhòu wǒ xiān shuā yá、

○ 康爱丽: 我每天六点一刻起床，起床以后我先刷牙、

xǐ liǎn, ránhòu chī zǎofàn, bā diǎn zuǒyòu lái xuéxiào. Nǐ ne?

洗脸，然后吃早饭，八点左右来学校。你呢？

Alice: I get up at a quarter past six. After getting up, I brush my teeth, wash my face and then have my breakfast. I come to school at about eight. What about you?

Kǎ'ěr: Wǒ yìbān bā diǎn guò wǔ fēn qǐchuáng, shuā yá、xǐzǎo, ránhòu lái jiàoshì.

● 卡尔: 我一般八点过五分起床，刷牙、洗澡，然后来教室。

Karl: I usually get up at five past eight. After getting up, I brush my teeth, wash my face, and then come to the classroom.

Kāng Àilì: Wǒmen bā diǎn bàn shàngkè, nǐ láidejí ma?

○ 康爱丽：我们八点半上课，你来得及吗？

Alice: We begin the class at half past eight. Do you have enough time for it?

Kǎ'ěr: Yǒushíhou láibují, suǒyǐ wǒ chángcháng chídào.

● 卡尔：有时候来不及，所以我常常迟到。

Karl: Sometimes I don't, so I'm often late.

Kāng Àilì: Nǐ wǎnshang jǐ diǎn shuìjiào?

○ 康爱丽：你晚上几点睡觉？

Alice: What time do you go to bed at night?

Kǎ'ěr: Yǒu shíhou zǎo, yǒu shíhou wǎn, yìbān liǎng diǎn zuǒyòu shuìjiào.

● 卡尔：有时候早，有时候晚，一般两点左右睡觉。

Karl: Sometimes early, and sometimes late. But I usually go to bed around two o'clock.

Kāng Àilì: Liǎng diǎn? Tài wǎn le!

○ 康爱丽：两点？太晚了！

Alice: Two o'clock? It's too late!

Kǎ'ěr: Méi bànfǎ! Zuòyè tài duō le!

● 卡尔：没办法！作业太多了！

Karl: I have no way out! I have so much homework!

生词 Shēngcí **New Words**

1. 起床	qǐ chuáng	V // O	to get up
2. 刻	kè	M	a quarter (of an hour)
3. 以后	yǐhòu	N	after, later
4. 先	xiān	Adv	first
5. 刷	shuā	V	to brush
6. 牙	yá	N	tooth
7. 洗	xǐ	V	to wash
8. 脸	liǎn	N	face
9. 然后	ránhòu	Conj	then

10. 吃	chī	V	to eat
11. 早饭	zǎofàn	N	breakfast
12. 八	bā	Nu	eight
13. 左右	zuǒyòu	N	about, around
14. 一般	yìbān	Adv	usually
15. 过	guò	V	past (expression of time)
16. 五	wǔ	Nu	five
17. 洗澡	xǐ zǎo	V // O	to have a shower
18. 教室	jiàoshì	N	classroom
19. 上课	shàng kè	V // O	to have a class
20. 来得及	láidejí	V	to have enough time (to do sth.)
21. 有时候	yǒushíhou	Adv	sometimes
22. 来不及	láibují	V	not to have enough time (to do sth.)
23. 所以	suǒyǐ	Conj	therefore, so
24. 常常	chángcháng	Adv	often
25. 睡觉	shuì jiào	V // O	to sleep
26. 早	zǎo	Adj	early
27. 晚	wǎn	Adj	late
28. 办法	bànfǎ	N	way, method
29. 作业	zuòyè	N	homework

注释 Zhùshì **Notes**

1 起床以后我先刷牙、洗脸，……　After getting up, I brush my teeth, wash my face…

"以后"，方位词。表示现在或所说的某个时间之后的时期。例如：

"以后", a locality noun, indicates a period of time in the future or after some time. For example,

VP/ TW	LN（以后），	Sentence
起床		我先刷牙，然后吃饭。
来中国	以后，	我在北京学习汉语。
八点		他开始工作。

2 我先刷牙、洗脸，然后吃早饭。

I brush my teeth, wash my face and then have my breakfast.

"先……，然后……"，用来表示事情、动作发生的顺序。例如：

"先……，然后……" indicates the sequence of actions. For example,

S	Adv（先）	VP₁	Conj（然后）	VP₂
我		刷牙，		洗澡。
卡尔	先	上课，	然后	去买东西。
他		做作业，		发邮件。
我们		吃饭，		看电影（diànyǐng，film）。

3 八点左右来学校。I come to school at about eight.

"左右"，方位词，用在数目字的后面，表示大概的数目。例如：

"左右" is a locality noun used after a number to indicate an approximate number. For example,

① 我每天十一点左右睡觉。

② 研讨会下午两点左右开始。

③ 他今年三十岁（suì, age）左右。

4 你来得及吗？ Do you have enough time for it?／有时候来不及。Sometimes I don't.

"来得及"，表示肯定，有足够的时间做某件事。例如：

"来得及" is used to indicates the speaker has enough time to do something. For example,

① 八点半上课，现在七点半，我们来得及吃早饭。

"来不及"，表示否定，时间不够，不能做某件事。

"来不及" indicates the speaker doesn't have enough time to do something.

它们可以单用，在句子中时，后面只能带动词或是动词短语。例如：

They can be used on their own and be followed only by a verb or a verbal phrase. For example,

②研讨会八点开始，现在已经七点五十五了，来不及了。

③他八点半上课，八点一刻起床，所以每天来不及吃饭。

④ 麦克（Màikè, Mike）在北京的时间太短（duǎn, short）了，来不及去长城（Chángchéng, the Great Wall）。

5 有时候来不及，所以我常常迟到。Sometimes I don't, so I'm often late.

"所以"，连词，表示因果关系，常跟连词"因为"连用。上一小句用"因为"表示原因，下一小句用"所以"表示结果。有时"因为"可以省略。例如：

"所以", a conjunction, indicates a causality. It is often used with another conjunction "因为". "因为" is used to denote the reason in the first clause, and "所以" is used to denote the result in the following clause. "因为" is omitted sometimes. For example,

①我想（xiǎng, would like）在中国工作，所以我来北京学习汉语。

②我们今天下午要参加研讨会，所以不来上课。

③我工作很忙，所以没时间去旅行（lǚxíng, to travel）。

④（因为）我常常迟到，所以老师很生气（shēng qì, to be angry）。

6 有时候早，有时候晚。Sometimes early, and sometimes late.

"有时候"，副词，表示偶尔。一般在句中作状语，修饰动词、形容词等。也可说"有时"。两个"有时候"连用，组成"有时候……，有时候……"结构，表示不同的现象或情况交替发生。例如：

"有时候", an adverb, indicates "sometimes". "有时" can also be used. It is generally used as an adverbial modifier modifying verbs, adjectives, etc. in a sentence. The commonly used structure is "有时候……，有时候……", indicating that different phenomena or situations happen alternatively. For example,

S	P			
	Adv（有时候）	……	Adv（有时候）	……
		早，		晚。
他	有时候	工作，	有时候	不工作。
我		八点起床		八点半起床。

7 **没办法！** **I have no way out!**

"没办法"，表示说话人很无奈，没有别的选择。可单独使用。例如：

"没办法" indicates that the speaker has no other options available. It can be used on its own. For example,

① 没办法，来不及了，火车（huǒchē, train）开走了。

（表示时间晚了 Indicating it's late）

② 没办法，老师下班（xià bān, to get off work）了。

（表示找不到老师了 Indicating someone cannot find the teacher）

③ 没办法，超市（chāoshì, supermarket）关门（guān mén, to close）了。

（表示不能买东西了 Indicating someone cannot go shopping）

④ 没办法，没有出租车（chūzūchē, taxi），迟到了。

Kǎ'ěr de Yì Tiān

卡尔的一天

One day of Karl's

Lái Zhōngguó yǐqián, Kǎ'ěr zài yì jiā diànnǎo gōngsī gōngzuò. Tā měi tiān

来中国以前，卡尔在一家电脑公司工作。他每天

shàngwǔ jiǔ diǎn shàngbān, xiàwǔ wǔ diǎn xiàbān, zhōngwǔ xiūxi yí ge xiǎoshí.

上午九点上班，下午五点下班，中午休息一个小时。

Cóng xīngqīyī dào xīngqīwǔ, tā qù gōngsī gōngzuò, zhōumò xiūxi.

从星期一到星期五，他去公司工作，周末休息。

Karl worked at a computer company before he came to China. He went to work at nine in the morning, and got off work at five in the afternoon, with one hour's break at noon. He went to work from Monday to Friday and took the weekend off.

生词 Shēngcí **New Words**

1.	以前	yǐqián	N	before, ago
2.	上午	shàngwǔ	N	morning
3.	九	jiǔ	Nu	nine
4.	上班	shàng bān	V∥O	to go to work
5.	下班	xià bān	V∥O	to get off work
6.	中午	zhōngwǔ	N	noon
7.	休息	xiūxi	V	to have a rest
8.	小时	xiǎoshí	N	hour
9.	从	cóng	Prep	from
10.	星期一	xīngqīyī	N	Monday
11.	到	dào	V	to arrive
12.	星期五	xīngqīwǔ	N	Friday
13.	周末	zhōumò	N	weekend

注释 Zhùshì **Notes**

1 来中国以前，卡尔在一家电脑公司工作。

Karl worked at a computer company before he came to China.

"以前"，方位词，表示现在或所说的某个时间之前的时期。可在"以前"的前面加时间词语；也可加动词或动词词组，表示后一句的动作是在前一句的动作之后发生的。例如：

"以前", a locality noun, indicates a period of time in the past or before some time. Before "以前", time words, verbs or verbal phrases can be used to indicate that the action in the second clause took place before the action in the first one. For example,

VP / TW	LN（以前），	Sentence
睡觉		我先洗澡。
来中国	以前，	康爱丽在一家贸易公司工作。
三天		我在上海。
		我每天跑步。

2 从星期一到星期五，他去公司工作。He went to work from Monday to Friday.

"从……到……"，既可表示时间，也可表示距离。"从"，介词，表示起点，常和"到"配合使用。

"从……到……" indicates time or distance. "从" is a preposition indicating the starting point. It usually collocates with "到".

（1）表示一段时间，从起点到终点。例如：

It indicates a period from the beginning to the end. For example,

① 我从星期一到星期五上班。

② 我们从八点半到十二点上课。

③ 从开学（kāi xué, term begins）到现在，他每天都迟到。

（2）表示距离，从某个地方到另一个地方。例如：

It indicates the distance from one place to another. For example,

④ 从德国到法国

⑤ 从上海到北京

⑥ 从我家到学校

3 从星期一到星期五，他去公司工作。He went to work from Monday to Friday.

（1）"星期"的表示法：

Expressions of the days of a week:

	Expression 1	Expression 2
Monday	星期一（xīngqīyī）	周一（zhōuyī）
Tuesday	星期二（xīngqī'èr）	周二（zhōu'èr）
Wednesday	星期三（xīngqīsān）	周三（zhōusān）
Thursday	星期四（xīngqīsì）	周四（zhōusì）

Friday	星期五（xīngqīwǔ）	周五（zhōuwǔ）
Saturday	星期六（xīngqīliù）	周六（zhōuliù）
Sunday	星期天（xīngqītiān）/ 星期日（xīngqīrì）	周日（zhōurì）

问 Question	答 Answer
今天星期几？	（今天）星期二。
明天星期几？	（明天）星期三。
五月六号星期几？	（五月六号）星期四。
七号星期几？	（七号）星期五。

（2）"年"的表示法：

Expressions of the year:

1620年	一六二零年	yī liù èr líng nián
1999年	一九九九年	yī jiǔ jiǔ jiǔ nián
2000年	二零零零年	èr líng líng líng nián
2009年	二零零九年	èr líng líng jiǔ nián
2010年	二零一零年	èr líng yī líng nián

（3）"月"的表示法：

Expressions of the month:

January	一月	yīyuè
February	二月	èryuè
March	三月	sānyuè
April	四月	sìyuè
May	五月	wǔyuè
June	六月	liùyuè
July	七月	qīyuè

August	八月	bāyuè
September	九月	jiǔyuè
October	十月	shíyuè
November	十一月	shíyīyuè
December	十二月	shí'èryuè

（4）"日"的表示法：

Expressions of the date:

汉语里表示日期时，常在数字后加上"日"或"号"。例如：

In Chinese, "日" or "号" is usually used after a number to denote the date. For example,

	Expression 1	Expression 2
6th	六号（liù hào）	六日（liù rì）
10th	十号（shí hào）	十日（shí rì）
20th	二十号（èrshí hào）	二十日（èrshí rì）

（5）年、月、日、星期的顺序：

The order of the week, month, date and year:

年	月	日	星期
1999年 一九九九年 yī jiǔ jiǔ jiǔ nián	3月 三月 sānyuè	20号 二十日 èrshí rì	Thursday 星期四 xīngqīsì
2000年 二零零零年 èr líng líng líng	6月 六月 liùyuè	6号 六号 liù hào	Sunday 星期天 xīngqītiān

练习 Liànxí Exercises

一 跟读生词,注意发音和声调。
Read the new words after the teacher and pay attention to your pronunciation.

二 跟读课文,注意语音语调。
Read the texts after the teacher and pay attention to your pronunciation.

三 学生分组,分角色朗读课文一、二、三。
Divide the students into groups and read Texts 1, 2 & 3 in roles.

四 学生分组,不看书,分角色表演课文一、二、三。
Divide the students into groups and play the roles in Texts 1, 2 & 3 without referring to the book.

五 角色扮演。(提示:角色可以互换。)
Role play. (Note: the roles can be exchanged.)

1. 一个学生扮演留学生 A,另一个学生扮演他的朋友 B。A 想请 B 一起去看电影,B 问 A 现在的时间、电影开始的时间,并且约定出发的时间。
Student A plays the role of an international student, and Student B acts as his friend. A wants to invite B to see a movie. B asks A about the present time, the time the movie starts and the time for them to set out.

2. 两个学生一组,用课文里的词语和句子互相询问:来中国以前和来中国以后每天的作息时间。
Two students as a group to ask and answer questions on their daily schedules before and after they came to China.

六 用汉语说出下面的日期。
Read the following dates in Chinese.

5th May, 1860   8th Aug, 1945   7th Jul, 1997

10th Sep, 2000   14th Oct, 2003   26th Nov, 2010

七 用 "二" 或者 "两" 填空。
Fill in the blanks with "二" or "两".

① 我有( )位辅导老师。

② 一、( )、三、四、五、六、七,这儿有七个数字。

③ 我每天六点( )十起床。

④ 我每天学习（　　　）个小时。

⑤ 我认识（　　　）个朋友。

⑥ 我有（　　　）张名片。

八 替换练习。
Substitution drills.

① A：现在几点?
　　B：现在　差两分一点。

一点过三分

四点一刻

十一点半

十七点三刻

二十点差五分

② 你　知道　现在几点　吗?

他是谁

她在哪儿

康爱丽是哪国人

卡尔在哪儿工作

③ 别　迟到!

问他

说话

去那儿

生气

④ 你 每天 几点 起床?

> 上课
>
> 下课（xià kè, to get out of class）
>
> 睡觉
>
> 上班
>
> 下班

⑤ 起床 以后，我 先刷牙、洗脸。

来中国	开始学习汉语
下课	去吃饭
下班	去买东西（mǎi dōngxi, to go shopping）
八点	在家

⑥ 我 先 刷牙，然后 吃早饭。

吃早饭	上课
上课	休息
回家	吃饭
去上海	去广州（Guǎngzhōu, name of a Chinese city）

⑦ 你 来得及 吃饭 吗?

> 洗脸
>
> 刷牙
>
> 上课
>
> 回家

⑧ 有时候 <u>早</u>，有时候 <u>晚</u>。

冷 （lěng, cold）	热
工作	学习
休息	不休息
在公司	在学校

⑨ 我 <u>两点</u> <u>左右</u> <u>睡觉</u>。

七点	起床
八点	开始上课
十二点	吃午饭 （wǔfàn, lunch）
下午四点	回家

⑩ <u>来中国</u> 以前，我 <u>在一家电脑公司工作</u>。

下班	得 （děi, to have to） 工作
下课	在教室学习
吃饭	先刷牙
来北京	没有中文名字

⑪ 从 <u>星期一</u> 到 <u>星期五</u> ，他 <u>去公司</u>。

星期六	星期天	休息
三点	五点	参加研讨会
上午九点	下午五点	工作
来中国以后	现在	在北京学习汉语

九 用下面的词语组成句子。
Make sentences with the following words and expressions.

1 没　表　戴　我

2 开始　的　几点　今天　中国经济研讨会　下午

3 了　你　准备　吗　好

4 快　你们　吧　去

5 起床　我　过　八点　一般　五分

6 来　八点　学校　左右　我

7 我　迟到　常常

8 多　太　作业　了

9 工作　电脑　一家　卡尔　公司　在

10 休息　小时　中午　个　一

十 完成对话。
Complete the dialogues.

1 A：请问，现在几点？

　　B：_____。

　　A：研讨会几点开始？

　　B：_____。

2 A：_____？

　　B：我每天七点起床。你呢？

99

A：_____。

B：你上课来得及吗?

A：_____。

③ A：你每天都十点睡觉吗?

B：_____。

十一 完成任务：请用课文中学过的词语和句子完成任务。
Complete the tasks: Please complete the tasks with the words and sentences you have learned in the texts.

---

1. 请调查：(1)中国公司的工作时间；比较中国公司和你们国家的公司的工作时间有什么不同。(2)普通中国学生每天的作息时间。

   Please survey: (1) What are the working hours at Chinese companies? What are the differences between Chinese companies and companies in your mother country? (2) What is the schedule of an ordinary Chinese student?

2. 请在上课时向老师和同学介绍你了解到的情况。

   Make a presentation in class about what you've learned.

第五单元
UNIT
买东西
Shopping

您要买什么
Can I help you

课文 Text	题目 Title	注释 Notes
一	您要买什么书 Can I help you	1. 能愿动词"要"　The optative verb"要" 2. 疑问代词"什么"　The interrogative pronoun"什么" 3. 能愿动词"想"　The optative verb"想" 4. 动词"看"　The verb"看" 5. 疑问代词"怎么样" 　　The interrogative pronoun"怎么样" 6. "又……又……" 7. 动词重叠　Reduplication of verbs 8. "不 A 不 B" 9. 副词"就"　The adverb"就" 10. 疑问代词"多少"　The interrogative pronoun"多少" 11. 人民币的计数　Numeration of RMB
二	苹果怎么卖 How much are these apples	1. "老板"、"师傅" 2. 疑问代词"怎么"　The interrogative pronoun"怎么" 3. 名词谓语句　The sentence with a nominal predicate 4. 动词"来"　The verb"来" 5. 数量词"一点儿"　The quantifier"一点儿" 6. "……，好吗？" 7. 动词"要"　The verb"要" 8. 副词"还"　The adverb"还" 9. 副词"一共"　The adverb"一共"
三	这件衣服挺好 看的 This coat is rather nice	1. "欢迎光临" 2. "挺 +Adj+ 的" 3. "的"字结构　The "的"-structure 4. 能愿动词"可以"　The optative verb"可以" 5. "你觉得……怎么样？" 6. 副词"有（一）点儿"　The adverb"有（一）点儿" 7. 副词"再"　The adverb"再" 8. "……号"

Nín yào Mǎi Shénme Shū

您要买什么书

Can I help you

Kāng Àilì zài shūdiàn mǎi shū.

康爱丽在书店买书。

Alice is buying a book in a bookshop.

Shòuhuòyuán: Nín yào mǎi shénme shū?
● 售货员： 您要买什么书？
Shop assistant: Can I help you?

Kāng Àilì: Wǒ xiǎng mǎi yì běn《Yīng-Hàn Cídiǎn》.
○ 康爱丽： 我想买一本《英汉词典》。
Alice:　　 I want to buy an English-Chinese dictionary.

Shòuhuòyuán: Nín kàn zhè běn cídiǎn zěnmeyàng?
● 售货员： 您看这本词典怎么样？
Shop assistant: What about this one?

Kāng Àilì: Zhè běn cídiǎn yòu dà yòu hòu, bù fāngbiàn.
○ 康爱丽： 这本词典又大又厚，不方便。
Alice:　　 It is too big and thick and it's not convenient for me to carry it around.

Shòuhuòyuán: Nín děngdeng! Wǒ bāng nín zhǎozhao.
● 售货员： 您等等！我帮您找找。
Shop assistant: Wait! Let me help you find another one.

Kāng Àilì: Xièxie!
○ 康爱丽： 谢谢！
Alice: Thank you.

Shòuhuòyuán: Bú kèqi!
● 售货员： 不客气！
Shop assistant: You are welcome!

Shòuhuòyuán yòu nálai yì běn cídiǎn.
售货员又拿来一本词典。
The shop assistant brings another dictionary to Alice.

Shòuhuòyuán: Zhè běn zěnmeyàng?
● 售货员： 这本怎么样？
Shop assistant: What about this one?

Kāng Àilì: Bú dà bù xiǎo, jiù mǎi zhè běn ba. Zhè běn cídiǎn duōshao qián?
○ 康爱丽： 不大不小，就买这本吧。这本词典多少钱？
Alice: It's neither too big nor too small. I'll take this one. How much is it?

Shòuhuòyuán: Èrshísì kuài wǔ.
● 售货员： 二十四块五。
Shop assistant: 24.5 *kuai*.

生词 Shēngcí **New Words**

1. 要	yào	OpV	to want
2. 买	mǎi	V	to buy
3. 书	shū	N	book
4. 售货员	shòuhuòyuán	N	shop assistant, salesclerk
5. 想	xiǎng	OpV	would like
6. 本	běn	M	*a measure word for books, etc.*

7. 英（语）	Yīng (yǔ)	N	English
8. 词典	cídiǎn	N	dictionary
9. 看	kàn	V	to look
10. 怎么样	zěnmeyàng	QPr	what about
11. 又……又……	yòu……yòu……		both…and…
12. 大	dà	Adj	big
13. 厚	hòu	Adj	thick
14. 方便	fāngbiàn	Adj	convenient
15. 等	děng	V	to wait
16. 帮	bāng	V	to help
17. 找	zhǎo	V	to look for
18. 不客气	bú kèqi	IE	You are welcome.
19. 小	xiǎo	Adj	small, little
20. 就	jiù	Adv	just
21. 多少	duōshao	QPr	how much, how many
22. 钱	qián	N	money
23. 二十四	èrshísì	Nu	twenty-four
24. 块	kuài	M	*a unit of Chinese currency*

注释　Zhùshì　**Notes**

1　您要买什么书？　**Can I help you?**

　　"要"，能愿动词，表示做某件事的意志，是主观的愿望和要求，必须放在动词前。例如：

　　"要"，an optative verb, indicates somebody wants to do something. It must be put before a verb.

For example,

S	P		
	OpV（要）	V	O
我		去	公园（gōngyuán, park）。
李明明		学	英语。
你	要	买	衣服（yīfu, clothes）吗？
他们		吃	什么？
你		去	哪儿？

这里的"要"的否定式一般用"不想、不愿意（yuànyì, would like to）"，不说"不要"。例如：

The negative form of "要" is "不想" or "不愿意"(yuànyì, would like to)", not "不要". For example,

问 Question	答 Answer
你要喝茶吗？	我不想喝茶。
你要考HSK吗？	我不想考HSK。

2 **您要买什么书？ Can I help you?**

"什么"，疑问代词，表疑问。用在名词前询问人或事物。例如：

"什么", an interrogative pronoun, indicates questioning. It is used before nouns to inquire about sb. or sth. For example,

① A: 他是什么人？

B: 他是我们的老师。

② 他想买什么书？

③ 你要问什么问题？

④ 你叫什么名字？

"什么"也可单用，用来询问事物。例如：

It can also be used on its own to inquire about things. For example,

⑤ 那是什么？

⑥ 你说什么？

⑦ 您找什么？

3 我想买一本《英汉词典》。I want to buy an English-Chinese dictionary.

"想"，这里是能愿动词，表示希望、打算等，须放在动词、形容词或句子前。前面可加表示程度的副词，如"很"。例如：

"想", an optative verb, indicates somebody's hope and plan, etc. It must be put before a verb, an adjective, or a sentence. An adverb of degree like "很" can be put before it. For example,

S	P		
	OpV（想）	V	O
张远		当	经理。
我		买	一个MP3。
他		回	国。
你	想	学习	汉语吗？
她		喝	什么？
你		买	几本词典？

4 你看这本词典怎么样？ What about this one?

"看"，动词，"认为"的意思，表示看法，后面常常带动词或者是小句作宾语。用在第二人称"你、你们"后询问别人的看法，用在第一人称"我、我们"后表达自己的看法。例如：

"看", a verb, indicates "think" here. It is used to ask for others' opinion when being put after the second-person pronoun "你" or "你们", or to express the speaker's own opinion when used after the first-person pronoun "我" or "我们". For example,

问 Question	答 Answer
你看这本书难吗？	我看（这本书）非常难。
你们看今天的作业多不多？	我看（今天的作业）不多。

5 你看这本词典怎么样？ What about this one?

"怎么样"，疑问代词，也可说"怎样"，在特指疑问句中用来询问性质、状况等，在句中作谓语。例如：

"怎么样" is an interrogative pronoun serving as a predicate to inquire the characteristics or situation in a special question. It is equivalent to "怎样". For example,

S	P
sth. / sb. / clause	QPr（怎么样）
这本书	
今天下午的研讨会	怎么样？
王老师	
我们去公园，	

"你看……怎么样"，用于询问意见、看法。例如：

"你看……怎么样" is used to inquire sb.'s suggestion or idea. For example,

你看	sth. / sb. / clause	QPr（怎么样）
你看	我的衣服	
	卡尔	怎么样？
	咱们去上海	

6 这本词典又大又厚。**It is too big and thick.**

"又……又……"，两个副词"又"连用，表示两种动作、状态同时存在或表示两种性质、情况同时存在。连用的两个结构或词语须性质相同，如果前一个"又"后是形容词，那么后一个"又"后也应该是形容词，须同时赞扬或者贬损，不能一褒一贬。例如：

"又……又……" indicates the co-existence of two actions, states, characteristics or situations. The two structures or words connected must have the same nature. If the preceding "又" is followed by an adjective, then the other "又" must also be followed by an adjective. The speaker either commend or belittle the both. For example,

S	P			
	又	Adj₁	又	Adj₂
房间		大		干净 (gānjìng, clean)。
我	又	渴（kě, thirsty）	又	饿 (è, hungry)。
衣服		小		贵。

7 您等等！我帮您找找。 **Wait! Let me help you find another one.**

动词重叠。"等等"、"找找"是单音节动词"等"、"找"的重叠形式。大多数动词可以重叠，表示动作的持续或重复。有时表示动作经历的时间短，有时带有尝试的意思，有时也表示轻松随意。单音节动词的重叠形式是"AA"、"A 一 A"，双音节动词的重叠形式是"ABAB"。动词的宾语放在重叠形式的后面。例如：

"等等" and "找找" are reduplicated forms of the monosyllable verbs "等" and "找". Most verbs can be reduplicated to indicate the continuation or repetition of the actions. It also indicates that the action is done in a short time, or tentatively, or in a relaxed manner. The reduplicated form of a monosyllable verb is "AA" or "A 一 A"; the reduplicated form of a bisyllable is "ABAB". The object of a verb is used after its reduplicated form. For example,

① 我能看（一）看这本书吗？
② 我太累（lèi, tired）了，要休息休息。
③ 您尝（cháng, to taste）尝，很甜（tián, sweet）！
④ 周末的晚上我常常听（tīng, to listen）听音乐（yīnyuè, music）、上上网。

8 不大不小。 **It's neither too big nor too small.**

"不 A 不 B"，A、B 为意思相对的单音节形容词，表示适中。例如：

"不A不B"："A" and "B" are a pair of monosyllable adjective antonyms, indicating "moderate". For example,

S	P			
	不	Adj₁	不	Adj₂
这本词典		大		小。
我的衣服	不	长（cháng, long）	不	短。
她		胖（pàng, fat）		瘦（shòu, thin）。

9 就买这本吧。I'll take this one.

"就"，副词，放在动词前表示强调，表明说话人态度坚决，不能更改，加强肯定的意思。如"就买这本吧"，表示买的人决定买这本，不是别的。在句末加上"吧"可以缓和语气。例如：

"就" is an adverb used before verbs to denote emphasis. It indicates that the speaker is determined. "就买这本吧" indicates that the speaker decides to buy this book, not other ones. "吧" can be used at the end of the sentence to soften the tone. For example,

① 就去上海吧。

（决定去上海，不去别的地方　Shanghai, not other places, is the place to go.）

② 就喝咖啡吧。

（决定喝咖啡，不喝别的饮料　Coffee, not other drinks, is to be drunk.）

③ 就坐在这儿。

（肯定要坐在这儿，不坐在别的地方　Here, not other places, is the place to be seated.）

10 这本词典多少钱？How much is it?

"多少"，疑问代词，用来询问数量。和"几"不同，任何数量都可用"多少"来提问。"多少"出现在名词前时可不用量词。"多少钱"专门用来询问价格。例如：

"多少" is an interrogative pronoun used to ask for quantity. In contrast to "几", it can be used to raise the question no matter how large the number is. There is not a measure word when "多少" is used before the noun. For example, "多少钱" is used specially to ask the price. For example,

① 你们学校有多少（个）人？

（问人的数量 It is used to ask the number of the people.）

② 这间教室有多少张桌子？

（问事物的数量 It is used to ask the quantity of sth.）

③ 这本书多少钱？（问价格 It is used to ask the price.）

11 二十四块五。24.5 *kuai*.

人民币的计数：

Numeration of RMB:

人民币的计算单位是"元（yuán）"、"角（jiǎo）"、"分（fēn）"，口语中常说"块"、"毛"、"分"。在口语中，当钱数不是整数时，末位的"毛"或"分"常常省略。当钱数大于10，而且是整数时，末位的"元（块）"可省略不说。例如：

The units of RMB are "元 (yuán)", "角 (jiǎo)" and "分 (fēn)". But in oral Chinese, "块" and "毛" instead of "元" and "角" are usually used. When the amount is not a whole number, "毛" or "分" at the last digit is often omitted in oral Chinese. When the amount is a whole number larger than 10, "元 (块)" at the last digit can also be omitted. For example,

	Expression	Note
5.00 元	五元 wǔ yuán 五块 wǔ kuài	10元及以下的,如果"元(块)"在末位,一定要说:钱数+元(块)。 When the amount is a whole number equal to or smaller than 10, we must say "the amount of money+元(块)".
10.00 元	十元 shí yuán 十块 shí kuài	
9.80 元	九元八角 jiǔ yuán bā jiǎo 九块八毛 jiǔ kuài bā máo 九块八 jiǔ kuài bā	末位的"角(毛)"可省略。 When "角(毛)" is the last unit, it can be omitted.
10.05 元	十元零五分 shí yuán líng wǔ fēn 十块零五分 shí kuài líng wǔ fēn 十块零五 shí kuài líng wǔ	末位的"分"可省略。 When "分" is the last unit, it can be omitted.
7.42 元	七元四角二分 qī yuán sì jiǎo èr fēn 七块四毛二分 qī kuài sì máo èr fēn 七块四毛二 qī kuài sì máo èr	末位的"分"可省略。 When "分" is the last unit, it can be omitted.
62.2 元	六十二元二角 liùshí'èr yuán èr jiǎo 六十二块二毛 liùshí'èr kuài èr máo 六十二块二 liùshí'èr kuài èr	末位的"角(毛)"可省略。 When "角(毛)" is the last unit, it can be omitted.
34.45 元	三十四元四角五分 sānshísì yuán sì jiǎo wǔ fēn 三十四块四毛五分 sānshísì kuài sì máo wǔ fēn 三十四块四毛五 sānshísì kuài sì máo wǔ	末位的"分"可省略。 When "分" is the last unit, it can be omitted.
24.00 元	二十四元 èrshísì yuán 二十四块 èrshísì kuài 二十四 èrshísì	10元以上的,如"元(块)"在末位时可省略不说。 When the amount is a whole number larger than 10 and "元(块)" is the last unit, it can be omitted.

Píngguǒ Zěnme Mài

苹果怎么卖

How much are these apples

Kǎ'ěr zài yì jiā shuǐguǒdiàn mǎi shuǐguǒ.

卡尔在一家水果店买水果。

Karl is buying fruit in a fruit store.

Kǎ'ěr: Lǎobǎn, píngguǒ zěnme mài?

● 卡尔：老板，苹果怎么卖？

Karl: Master, how much are these apples?

Lǎobǎn: Sān kuài wǔ yì jīn. Lái yìdiǎnr ma?

○ 老板： 三块五一斤。来一点儿吗？

Shopkeeper: 3.5 *kuai* a *jin* (half a kilo). Do you want some?

Kǎ'ěr: Tài guì le, piányi diǎnr ba! Sān kuài yì jīn, hǎo ma?

● 卡尔：太贵了，便宜点儿吧！三块一斤，好吗？

Karl: Too expensive. Can it be cheaper? Is 3 *kuai* a *jin* OK?

Lǎobǎn: Hǎo ba. Nín yào duōshao?

○ 老板： 好吧。您要多少？

Shopkeeper: OK. How many do you want?

Kǎ'ěr: Lái wǔ ge.
● 卡尔：来五个。
Karl: I want five.

Lǎobǎn: Nín hái yào bié de ma?
○ 老板： 您还要别的吗？
Shopkeeper: What else do you want?

Kǎ'ěr: Bú yào le. Duōshao qián?
● 卡尔：不要了。多少钱？
Karl: Nothing. How much?

Lǎobǎn: Yígòng sān jīn, jiǔ kuài qián.
○ 老板： 一共三斤，九块钱。
Shopkeeper: 9 *kuai* for 3 *jin* in total.

Kǎ'ěr: Gěi nǐ qián.
● 卡尔：给你钱。
Karl: Here you are.

Kǎ'ěr gěile yìbǎi kuài.
卡尔给了一百块。
Karl gives the man 100 *kuai*.

Lǎobǎn: Zhǎo nín jiǔshíyī.
○ 老板： 找您九十一。
Shopkeeper: Here is your change, 91 *kuai*.

生词 Shēngcí **New Words**

1. 苹果	píngguǒ	N	apple
2. 卖	mài	V	to sell
3. 老板	lǎobǎn	N	boss, shopkeeper, master
4. 三	sān	Nu	three
5. 斤	jīn	M	*jin* (half a kilogram)
6. 来	lái	V	to buy

7. 一点儿	yìdiǎnr	Nu	a little, a bit
8. 贵	guì	Adj	expensive
9. 便宜	piányi	Adj	cheap
10. 要	yào	V	to need, to want
11. 还	hái	Adv	still
12. 别的	bié de		else
13. 一共	yígòng	Adv	in total
14. 找	zhǎo	V	to give change
15. 九十一	jiǔshíyī	Nu	ninty-one

注释 Zhùshì Notes

1 老板，苹果怎么卖？ Master, how much are these apples?

"老板"，是顾客对卖东西的人的客气的称呼，有时也称"师傅"。坐车、买东西或请人帮助时，不管男女，都可用"师傅"来称呼对方，不过，"师傅"常用来称呼年纪大一点儿的人。例如：

"老板" is a polite form of address to the retailer by customers, and "师傅" is also used sometimes. When taking a bus or taxi, or asking a favor of sb., we can call them "师傅" regardless of their gender. However, "师傅" is often used to refer to the aged. For example,

① 师傅，买一斤苹果。

② 师傅，去经贸大学怎么走？

2 苹果怎么卖？ How much are these apples?

"怎么"，疑问代词。"怎么卖"或"sth. + 怎么卖"，都表示询问价格，和"……多少钱"相同。

"怎么" is an interrogative pronoun. "怎么卖" or "sth. + 怎么卖" is used to inquire the price, similar to "……多少钱".

3 三块五一斤。3.5 *kuai* a *jin* (half a kilo).

名词谓语句。汉语里，名词、名词短语或数量短语可直接作句子的谓语，句中不用动词

"是"。但是这种谓语是有条件的，一般表示时间、天气、年龄、事物的价格、人或事物的数量等。多用在口语中，一般是肯定形式。例如：

This is a noun-predicate sentence. Nouns, noun phrases or quantifier phrases can directly serve as the predicate in a sentence, and the verb "是" is not needed. However, such a predicate is conditional. It usually denotes time, weather, age of people, price, or quantity, etc. It is often used in oral Chinese in the affirmative form. For example,

S	P
五毛	一本。
十块钱	三斤。
卡尔	（今年）三十岁。
我	三十二。（表示年龄 *indicating age*）
今天	星期六。
明天	多云（duōyún, cloudy）。

4 来一点儿吗？ **Do you want some?**／来五个。**I want five.**

"来"，动词，在句中代替其他意义更具体的动词，表示做某个动作。口语中，在饭馆或商店等地方，常用"来"表示"买"，前面的主语常省略。例如：

"来" is a verb used in a sentence to replace other words with more specific meanings to denote an action. In oral Chinese, "来" means "买 (to buy)" when it is used in a restaurant or store, and the preceding subject is often omitted. For example,

① 来两瓶（píng, bottle）水。

（在商店或饭店买水　Buying water in a store or restaurant）

② 来（一）杯咖啡。

（在酒吧、咖啡厅等地买咖啡　Buying coffee in a bar or coffee house）

③ 来一份（fèn, share）冰淇淋（bīngqílín, ice cream）。

④（您）来点儿什么？

5 来一点儿吗？ **Do you want some？**／便宜点儿吧！**Can it be cheaper?**

"一点儿"，数量词，表示数量不定且少。

"一点儿", a quantifier, indicates an uncertain amount which is usually small.

（1）可用在名词前作定语，当说话双方都知道是什么事物时，名词可省略。有时"一"

也可省略。例如：

It can be used before a noun as an attribute and the noun can be omitted if both parties know what they are referring to. "一" can also be omitted sometimes. For example,

① 你要来（一）点儿（苹果）吗？

② 他喝了（一）点儿酒（jiǔ, alcohol）。

③ 我会说（一）点儿汉语。

（2）"一点儿" 还可用在形容词后，表示程度低，轻微的。"一" 可省略。例如：

"一点儿", used after the adjective, means "a little bit". "一" can be omitted. For example,

④ 声音能大（一）点儿吗？

⑤ 能便宜（一）点儿吗？

⑥ 请您慢一点儿说。

6 三块一斤，好吗？ Is 3 *kuai* a *jin* OK?

"好吗"，放在句子末尾，用来提出建议或征询对方意见。前面的一般陈述句表示说话人的意见、建议。回答时常用 "好"、"好啊"、"可以" 表示肯定。基本结构：陈述句 + 好吗。例如：

"好吗" is used at the end of a sentence to put forward a suggestion, or ask the other party's opinion. The preceding declarative sentence denotes the idea or suggestion of the speaker. The affirmative answer to this sentence can be "好"，"好啊" or "可以". The basic structure is "declarative sentence + 好吗". For example,

Declarative sentence	好吗
咱们明天中午见面（jiàn miàn, to meet），	
咱们去尝尝北京烤鸭（kǎoyā, roast duck），	好吗？
请给我一张名片，	

7 您要多少？ How many do you want?

"要"，动词，"需要" 的意思。否定式是 "不要"。例如：

"要" is a verb which means "want or need". Its negative form is "不要". For example,

① 我要三斤（苹果）。

② 我不要苹果，我要香蕉（xiāngjiāo, banana）。

8 您还要别的吗？ **What else do you want?**

"还"，副词，表示某种情况继续存在，动作继续进行。例如：

"还", an adverb, indicates that a situation continues to exist or an action is going on. For example,

S	P		
	Adv（还）	V	O
您		买	什么？
我		要	两斤香蕉。
他	还	要去	哪儿？
你		想说	什么？
卡尔		在	中国。

"您还要别的吗"，是询问对方在已有的事物和要求之外，有没有其他的要求或需要。在买卖当中，卖者常用这样的句子追问、提示买者。

This sentence is used to ask the other party whether he/she still has other requests or needs. It is often used by sellers to prompt buyers to buy more things.

9 一共三斤，九块钱。 **9 *kuai* for 3 *jin* in total.**

"一共"，副词，表示合在一起。后面一定要有数量词或表示数量的疑问代词。例如：

"一共", an adverb, means "in total". There must be a quantifier or interrogative pronouns denoting amount after it. For example,

①A: 你们班一共多少人？

B: 我们班一共九个学生。

②A: 这些苹果一共多少钱？

B: 一共三十（块钱）。

Zhè Jiàn Yīfu Tǐng Hǎokàn de
这件衣服挺好看的
This coat is rather nice

Kǎ'ěr zài yì jiā fúzhuāngdiàn mǎi yīfu.

卡尔在一家服装店买衣服。

Karl is buying clothes in a clothing store.

Lǎobǎn:　　Huānyíng guānglín! Qǐng suíbiàn kànkan.

● 老板：　　欢迎光临！请随便看看。

Shopkeeper: Welcome! Please feel free to have a look.

Kǎ'ěr: Zhè jiàn yīfu tǐng hǎokàn de. Yǒu hēisè de ma?

○ 卡尔：这件衣服挺好看的。有黑色的吗？

Karl:　　This coat is rather nice. Do you have black ones?

Lǎobǎn:　　Méiyǒu, yǒu huī de、bái de、lán de……dōu tǐng hǎokàn de.

● 老板：　　没有，有灰的、白的、蓝的……都挺好看的。

Shopkeeper: No, but we have gray ones, white ones, blue ones… and they all look great.

Kǎ'ěr: Wǒ kěyǐ shìshi huī de ma?

○ 卡尔：我可以试试灰的吗？

Karl:　　May I try a gray one?

117

Lǎobǎn: Kěyǐ, gěi nín.
● 老板: 可以，给您。
Shopkeeper: Certainly, here you are.

Kǎ'ěr shì chuān hòu.
卡尔试穿后。
After trying on.

Kǎ'ěr: Nǐ juéde zěnmeyàng?
○ 卡尔：你觉得怎么样？
Karl: What do you think?

Lǎobǎn: Yǒudiǎnr xiǎo. Nín zài shìshi zhè jiàn dàhào de ba.
● 老板: 有点儿小。您再试试这件大号的吧。
Shopkeeper: A little bit small. You can try this large one.

Kǎ'ěr: Tǐng héshì de, jiù mǎi zhè jiàn ba.
○ 卡尔：挺合适的，就买这件吧。
Karl: This one fits well. I'll take it.

生词 Shēngcí New Words

1. 件	jiàn	M	a measure word for clothes, gifts, matters, etc.
2. 衣服	yīfu	N	clothes
3. 挺	tǐng	Adv	very, rather
4. 好看	hǎokàn	Adj	good-looking, nice
5. 光临	guānglín	V	to be present (of a guest, etc.)
6. 随便	suíbiàn	Adj	random, casual
7. 黑色	hēisè	N	black
8. 灰	huī	Adj	gray
9. 白	bái	Adj	white
10. 蓝	lán	Adj	blue

11. 可以	kěyǐ	OpV	can, may
12. 试	shì	V	to try
13. 觉得	juéde	V	to feel, to think
14. 有点儿	yǒudiǎnr	Adv	a bit, a little
15. 再	zài	Adv	again, once more
16. 大号	dàhào	Adj	large size
17. 合适	héshì	Adj	suitable

注释 Zhùshì **Notes**

1 欢迎光临！Welcome！

"欢迎光临"，商家对顾客表示欢迎的礼貌用语。我们还可以在商店、宾馆、饭店等进门的门上和地毯上看到"欢迎光临"的字样。

This is a polite expression often used to welcome guests. On the door or the carpet on the floor at the entrance of a shop, hotel or restaurant, the characters "欢迎光临" are often seen.

2 这件衣服挺好看的！This coat is rather nice！

"挺 + Adj + 的"，用来肯定事物性质达到了形容词表示的程度。"挺"，副词，"很"的意思，表程度。可用在口语中，在形容词前作状语。"的"，用在陈述句末尾表示肯定语气。例如：

"挺 + Adj + 的" is used to indicate the quality of sth. has reached a degree described by the adjective. "挺" is an adverb which means "很". It indicates the degree. It can be used as an adverbial in oral Chinese and followed by an adjective. "的" is used at the end of a declarative sentence to indicate affirmation. For example,

① 他会生气的。
② 你会学好汉语的。
③ 他学习挺努力（nǔlì, to make great efforts）的。
④ 苹果挺甜的。

3 有灰的、白的、蓝的…… We have gray ones, white ones, blue ones…

"的"字结构。"的"，助词。"名词、代词、动词、形容词、主谓短语 + 的"构成"的"字结构。"的"字结构相当于名词,表示已知的、具体的人或事物,出现在一定的语境中。在句中可以作主语、宾语。"的"字后省略了根据上下文可以知道或双方已经知道的人或事物。例如:

In the "的"-structure, "的" is an auxiliary. The structure of "a noun, pronoun, verb, an adjective or a subject-predicate phrase + 的" equals to a noun, indicating that sb. or sth. appears in a certain context. It is used as a subject or an object in a sentence. The part after "的" which can be known from the context or is known to both the speaker and listener is omitted. For example,

① 有白的吗?(白的 = 白的衣服   white one = white garment)

② 这个苹果是我的。(我的 = 我的苹果   mine = my apple)

③ 红(hóng, red)的是她的书包(shūbāo, schoolbag)。

　　(红的 = 红的书包   red one = the red bag)

4 **我可以试试灰的吗? May I try a gray one?**

"可以",能愿动词,用在动词前,这里表示情理上许可。例如:

"可以", an optative verb, is used before verbs to indicate "permission". For example,

① 今天我没有课,你可以来我家。

② 晚上我们可以上网。

这时,陈述句中"可以"的否定形式通常用"不能"。例如:

"不能" can be usually used for a negative answer in a declarative sentence. For example,

③ 这本书不能再便宜了。

④ 这儿不能打(dǎ, to play)篮球(lánqiú, basketball)。

"可以"可单独回答问题。这时,肯定形式用"可以",否定形式用"不行(bùxíng, no)",不用"不可以"。例如:

"可以" can be used as an answer on its own. It this case, its affirmative form is "可以" and its negative form is "不行". "不可以" cannot be used. For example,

问 Question	答 Answer
我可以看看你的书吗?	可以。
你的电话号码(hàomǎ, number)可以给我吗?	可以。
可以尝尝吗?	可以。
上课可以打电话吗?	不行。
今天的作业可以不做吗?	不行。
我下午可以去商店吗?	不行,你得来上课。

5 你觉得怎么样? **What do you think?**

"你觉得(+sth. /sb. / VP/ clause)+ 怎么样",用来询问别人的看法。例如:

It is used to ask for the other party's opinion. "你觉得 +sth. /sb. / VP/ clause+ 怎么样" can also be used. For example,

你觉得	sth. /sb. / VP/ clause	QPr(怎么样)
你觉得	这件衣服	怎么样?
	他	
	买这件	
	我们晚上去看电影	

6 有点儿小。**A little bit small.**

"有(一)点儿",副词,表示程度不高,稍微。用在动词、形容词前,只能作状语。可表示评价,常带有不如意的意思。"一"常省略。例如:

"有(一)点儿", an adverb, means "a little bit". It is used before verbs or adjectives in a sentence as an adverbial modifier to indicate that sb. or sth. is not quite satisfying. "一" is often omitted. For example,

S	P	
	Adv(有点儿)	Adj
那件衣服	有点儿	大。
我		忙。
他		胖。
汉字		难。
我们		想去上海。

"有(一)点儿"可单独回答问题。例如:

It can also be used on its own as an answer. For example,

①A: 你忙吗?

B: 有(一)点儿。

②A: 你觉得热吗？

　B: 有（一）点儿。

7 您再试试这件大号的吧。You can try this large one.

"再"，副词，"又一次"的意思，表示将要重复的动作。例如：

"再" is an adverb which means "again". It denotes an action that will be repeated. For example,

①你再看看。

②苹果很甜，再来两斤。

③我明天再来。

④我还不懂（dǒng, to understand），老师，请再讲一遍（biàn, time），好吗？

8 您再试试这件大号的吧。You can try this large one.

"……号"，表示衣服的大小。例如：

"……号" indicates the size of clothes. For example,

S号	M号	L号	XL号
小号	中号	大号	特大号
xiǎohào	zhōnghào	dàhào	tèdàhào

有时也用"数字＋号"，如"39号"、"41号"。

"Number ＋ 号" is also used sometimes, such as "39 号", "41 号".

鞋的大小也可用"数字＋号"表示。例如：

"Number ＋ 号" can also be used to indicate the size of shoes. For example,

36号（23cm）	37号（23.5cm）	38号（24cm）	40号（25cm）
6号（24cm）	7号（25cm）	8号（26cm）	10号（28cm）

一 跟读生词,注意发音和声调。
Read the new words after the teacher and pay attention to your pronunciation.

二 跟读课文,注意语音语调。
Read the texts after the teacher and pay attention to your pronunciation.

三 学生分组,分角色朗读课文一、二、三。
Divide the students into groups and read Texts 1, 2 & 3 in roles.

四 学生分组,不看书,分角色表演课文一、二、三。
Divide the students into groups and play the roles in Texts 1, 2 & 3 without referring to the book.

五 根据课文,回答下面的问题。
Answer the following questions according to the texts.

教师提问,学生集体回答。然后两个学生一组,互相提问并回答。
The teacher raises a question, and the students answer it together. Then students work in pairs to ask and answer questions in turn.

1. 课文一的问题: The questions about Text 1:

① 康爱丽去哪儿买东西?

② 康爱丽买了什么? 那本词典怎么样?

③ 她花了多少钱?

2. 课文二的问题: The questions about Text 2:

① 卡尔去水果店买什么?

② 苹果怎么样?

③ 多少钱一斤?

④ 卡尔买了多少苹果?

⑤ 卡尔花了多少钱?

3. 课文三的问题: The questions about Text 3:

① 卡尔去买什么?

② 衣服有什么颜色的?

③ 卡尔买了什么样的衣服?

④ 卡尔试穿了几次?

六 角色扮演。（提示：角色可以互换。）
Role play. (Note: the roles can be exchanged.)

1. 关于价格：两人一组，用所给的词语提问，用所给的价格回答。
   Ask the price: Students work in pairs. One raises questions with the given words, and the other answers with the given prices.

A	B
苹果怎么卖？	三块五一斤。
……（衣服）？	……（298）。
……（面包）？	……（16.3）。
……（手机 shǒujī, mobile phone）？	……（1740）。
……（眼镜 yǎnjìng, glasses）？	……（142）。

2. 描述人或物品：两人一组，用所给的词语互相问答，练习句型"……怎么样"和"又……又……"。
   Describe people or articles: Students work in pairs to ask and answer questions in turn. Practice the sentence patterns："……怎么样" and "又……又……".

A	B
这本词典怎么样？	这本词典又大又厚。
……（儿子）？	……（高 gāo, tall／胖）。
……（房间）？	……（大／干净）。
……（苹果）？	……（大／甜）。
……（头发 tóufa, hair）？	……（黑／长）。

3. 关于比较：两人一组，用所给的词语完成对话。
   Compare: Students work in pairs to complete the dialogues with the given words.

A	B
苹果太贵了！	有便宜一点儿的吗？
……（难）！	……（容易 róngyì, easy）？
……（快）！	……（慢 màn, slow）？
……（多）！	……（少）？
……（大）！	……（小）？

4. 关于评价：两人一组，用"怎么样"提问，用提示的词语和"有点儿"回答。
Evaluate: Students work in pairs to ask questions with "怎么样" and answer the questions with the given words and "有点儿".

A	B
衣服怎么样？	衣服有点儿小。
……？	…… (忙)。
……？	…… (累)。
咖啡……？	…… (苦 kǔ, bitter)。
……？	…… (热)。

5. 关于买东西：两位或三位同学一组，分别扮演售货员和顾客，模拟表演买水果、买衣服或买其他物品。
Go shopping: Two or three students work as a group to act out shop assistants and customers as if they were buying fruit, clothes or other articles.

七 复述课文：按照例文，复述课文二、课文三。
Retell the texts: Retell Texts 2 & 3 following the example.

例文　Example:

　　课文一中，康爱丽去书店买书，她想买一本《英汉词典》。有的词典又大又厚，不方便。康爱丽买了一本词典，二十四块五。那本词典很方便，不大不小。

八 替换练习。
Substitution drills.

① 您 要 买 什么？

你	喝
他	看
她	点（diǎn, toorder）
你们	听

② 我 想 买 一本 《英汉词典》。

他	点	两杯	啤酒
卡尔	喝	一瓶	可乐（kělè, cola）
老师	喝		绿茶（lǜchá, green tea）
我们	点		冰水（bīngshuǐ, ice water）

③ 我 想 买 词典。

我	逛（guàng, to stroll）	商店
她	看	电影
老板	打	高尔夫球（gāo'ěrfūqiú, golf）
妈妈	去	旅行
客户	参观（cānguān, to visit）	工厂（gōngchǎng, factory）

④ 苹果 怎么卖/多少钱？

香蕉

橘子（júzi, orange）

冰淇淋

咖啡

⑤ 你看 这本 词典 怎么样？

这本		书
这部（bù, a measure word for movies, etc.）		电影
那个		饭店
那辆（liàng, a measure word for cars, etc.）		汽车（qìchē, car）

6 明天　去　上海，好吗／怎么样？

七点	发	邮件
星期六	去	爬山（pá shān, to climb a mountain）
晚上	看	电影
周末	听	音乐会（yīnyuèhuì, concert）

7 你　再试试　这件　大号的。

我 看看	这本	书
你 听听	那首（shǒu, *a measure word for songs, etc.*)	歌（gē, song）
你 尝尝	这个	菜（cài, dish）
我 用（yòng, to use）用	你的	自行车（zìxíngchē, bike）

九 用下面的词语组成句子。
Make sentences with the following words and expressions.

1 什么　您　买　书　要

2 钱　多少　词典　这本

3 卖　怎么　苹果

4 三　一共　斤

5 别的　要　您　还　吗

6 九十一　您　找

⑦ 这件　挺　好看　衣服　的

⑧ 我　试试　灰的　可以　吗

⑨ 怎么样　觉得　你

⑩ 看　随便　请　看

⑪ 就　这件　买　吧

✚ 完成对话。
Complete the dialogues.

1. 卡尔在商店买东西。Karl is shopping.

售货员：您要_____什么？

卡　尔：我_____买_____。

售货员：您看这种_____？

卡　尔：_____。

售货员：还要别的吗？

卡　尔：不要了。一共_____？

售货员：_____块钱。

2. 卡尔在服装店买衣服。Karl is buying clothes in a clothing shop.

老板：欢迎_____！请随便_____。

卡　尔：_____挺好看的！有_____色的吗？

老板：有，还有_____色、_____色的。

卡　尔：我可以_____白色的吗？

老板：_____，给您。

卡　尔：我觉得_____小。我_____这件大号的。

（卡尔试穿后）

老板：挺_____。

3. 卡尔和康爱丽在教室聊天儿。Karl and Alice are chatting in the classroom.

卡　尔：最近你_____？

康爱丽：我有点儿_____，想休息休息。

卡　尔：我常常在家看看_____，听听_____，_____游戏（yóuxì，game）。

康爱丽：好，我也试试。

十一 完成任务：请用课文中学过的词语和句子完成任务。
Complete the tasks: Please complete the following tasks with the words and sentences you have learned in the texts.

1. 询价：请到附近的商店或市场询问并记录以下物品的价格，到课堂上向老师和同学报告；同时说明这些物品在你们国家的价格。
Price inquiry: Go to the shops or markets nearby for an investigation and write down the prices of articles, and report to your teacher and classmates in class. Tell the prices of the same articles in your country.

苹果　　　　　　　　　　草莓（cǎoméi，strawberry）

西瓜（xīguā，watermelon）　西红柿（xīhóngshì，tomato）

洋葱（yángcōng，onion）　　土豆（tǔdòu，potato）

黄瓜（huángguā，cucumber）　拖鞋（tuōxié，slippers）

短裤（duǎnkù，shorts）　　太阳镜（tàiyángjìng，sunglasses）

T恤衫（T xù shān，T-shirt）

2. 两人一组，到附近的市场观察中国人怎么买东西，到课堂上向老师和其他同学介绍下面的情况：
Two students working as a group go to the markets nearby to observe how Chinese people shop and then report to the teacher and classmates the following information:

(1) 他们买了什么东西？他们怎么问价钱？卖东西的人怎么回答？
What did they buy? How did they inquire about the prices? How did the sellers answer them?

(2) 请用拼音记录至少三个课文以外的新词语和句子。
Please use *pinyin* to write down at least three new words and sentences that are not learned in the texts.

生词总表
VOCABULARY

（最后一列表示生词所在单元和课号，如"032"表示第三单元课文二）

（The last column indicates the unit number and text number of the new word, for example, "032" indicatas the new word is in Text 2, Unit 3. ）

A					
1	啊	a	MdPt	*a particle used to strengthen the tone*	033
2	哎	āi	MdPt	*a particle used to remind of sth.*	023
B					
3	八	bā	Nu	eight	042
4	吧	ba	MdPt	*a particle to indicate suggestion and soften the tone of the sentence*	022
5	白	bái	Adj	white	053
6	办法	bànfǎ	N	way, method	042
7	半	bàn	Nu	half	041
8	帮	bāng	V	to help	051
9	抱歉	bàoqiàn	Adj	sorry	032
10	本	běn	M	*a measure word for books, etc.*	051
11	表	biǎo	N	watch	041
12	别	bié	Adv	don't	041
13	别的	bié de		else	052
14	不客气	bú kèqi	IE	You are welcome.	051
15	不	bù	Adv	no, not	022
C					
16	差	chà	V	to (*indicating that there is a certain amount of time before a particular time*)	041
17	常常	chángcháng	Adv	often	042
18	吃	chī	V	to eat	042
19	迟到	chídào	V	to be late	041

20	词典	cídiǎn	N	dictionary	051
21	从	cóng	Prep	from	043

D

22	大	dà	Adj	big	051
23	大号	dàhào	Adj	large size	053
24	戴	dài	V	to wear	041
25	当	dāng	V	to serve as	032
26	当然	dāngrán	Adv	of course, certainly	033
27	到	dào	V	to arrive	043
28	的	de	StPt	*a possessive or modifying particle*	011
29	等	děng	V	to wait	051
30	地方	dìfang	N	place, area	022
31	点	diǎn	M	o'clock	041
32	电脑	diànnǎo	N	computer	032
33	都	dōu	Adv	both, all	021
34	对	duì	Adj	yes, right, correct	031
35	多	duō	Adj	many, much	031
36	多少	duōshao	QPr	how much, how many	051

E

37	二十四	èrshísì	Nu	twenty-four	051

F

38	发	fā	V	to send	033
39	方便	fāngbiàn	Adj	convenient	051
40	非常	fēicháng	Adv	very much	033
41	分	fēn	M	minute	041
42	辅导	fǔdǎo	V	to coach, to tutor	021

G

43	高兴	gāoxìng	Adj	happy	011
44	告诉	gàosu	V	to tell	032
45	个	gè	M	*a common measure word*	022
46	给	gěi	V/Prep	to give; to, for	033
47	工作	gōngzuò	V/N	to work; job	032
48	公司	gōngsī	N	company	032
49	公寓	gōngyù	N	apartment	023
50	光临	guānglín	V	to be present (of a guest, etc.)	053
51	贵	guì	Adj	expensive	052
52	贵姓	guìxìng	N	(honorable) surname	012
53	国	guó	N	country, nation	021
54	过	guò	V	past (expression of time)	042
55	过来	guòlai	V	to come up	022

H

56	还	hái	Adv	passably, fairly	033
57	还	hái	Adv	still	052
58	汉语	Hànyǔ	N	Chinese languege	031
59	汉字	Hànzì	N	Chinese characters	031
60	好	hǎo	Adj	good	011
61	好看	hǎokàn	Adj	good-looking, nice	053
62	合适	héshì	Adj	suitable	053
63	黑色	hēisè	N	black	053
64	很	hěn	Adv	very	011
65	厚	hòu	Adj	thick	051
66	欢迎	huānyíng	V	to welcome	012
67	灰	huī	Adj	gray	053

J

68	几	jǐ	Nu	how many	041
69	家	jiā	M	*a measure word*	032
70	见	jiàn	V	to see	012
71	件	jiàn	M	*a measure word for clothes, gifts, matters, etc.*	053
72	叫	jiào	V	to call	011
73	教室	jiàoshì	N	classroom	042
74	节	jié	M	*a measure word*	031
75	斤	jīn	M	*jin (half a kilogram)*	052
76	今天	jīntiān	N	today	041
77	进	jìn	V	to come in	013
78	经济	jīngjì	N	economy	041
79	经理	jīnglǐ	N	manager	013
80	九	jiǔ	Nu	nine	043
81	九十一	jiǔshíyī	Nu	ninty-one	052
82	就	jiù	Adv	just	051
83	觉得	juéde	V	to feel, to think	053

K

84	开始	kāishǐ	V	to begin, to start	041
85	看	kàn	V	to look	051
86	可是	kěshì	Conj	but	031
87	可以	kěyǐ	OpV	can, may	053
88	刻	kè	M	a quarter (of an hour)	042
89	客户	kèhù	N	client	033
90	课	kè	N	class, lesson	031
91	块	kuài	M	*a unit of Chinese currency*	051
92	快	kuài	Adj	fast	041

L

93	来	lái	V	to come	012
94	来	lái	V	to buy	052
95	来不及	láibují	V	not to have enough time (to do sth.)	042
96	来得及	láidejí	V	to have enough time (to do sth.)	042
97	蓝	lán	Adj	blue	053
98	老板	lǎobǎn	N	boss, shopkeeper, master	052
99	老师	lǎoshī	N	teacher	012
100	了	le	Pt	*a particle*	033
101	脸	liǎn	N	face	042
102	两	liǎng	Nu	two	041
103	留学生	liúxuéshēng	N	international student	031
104	六	liù	Nu	six	031

M

105	吗	ma	QPt	*a particle*	011
106	买	mǎi	V	to buy	051
107	卖	mài	V	to sell	052
108	忙	máng	Adj / V	busy; to be busy	033
109	贸易	màoyì	N	trade	032
110	没	méi	Adv	not	041
111	没关系	méi guānxi	IE	It doesn't matter.	032
112	没有	méiyǒu	V	not	032
113	每	měi	Pr	every	031
114	名片	míngpiàn	N	business card	032
115	名字	míngzi	N	name	011
116	明天	míngtiān	N	tomorrow	041

N

117	哪	nǎ / něi	QPr	which	021
118	哪儿	nǎr	QPr	where	023
119	那	nà / nèi	Pr	that	021
120	难	nán	Adj	difficult	031
121	呢	ne	MdPt	*a modal particle*	012
122	能	néng	OpV	can	032
123	你	nǐ	Pr	you	011
124	你们	nǐmen	Pr	you	031
125	您	nín	Pr	you (respectful form)	012

P

126	朋友	péngyou	N	friend	021
127	便宜	piányi	Adj	cheap	052
128	苹果	píngguǒ	N	apple	052

Q

129	起床	qǐ chuáng	V∥O	to get up	042
130	钱	qián	N	money	051
131	请	qǐng	V	please	013
132	请问	qǐngwèn	V	excuse me	013
133	去	qù	V	to go	041

R

134	然后	ránhòu	Conj	then	042
135	人	rén	N	person, people	021
136	认识	rènshi	V	to know	011

S

| 137 | 三 | sān | Nu | three | 052 |

138	上班	shàng bān	V//O	to go to work	043
139	上课	shàng kè	V//O	to have a class	042
140	上网	shàng wǎng	V//O	to surf the Internet	033
141	上午	shàngwǔ	N	morning	043
142	谁	shéi / shuí	QPr	who, whom	021
143	什么	shénme	QPr	what	011
144	生意	shēngyi	N	business	033
145	是	shì	V	to be	011
146	市场	shìchǎng	N	market	033
147	事(儿)	shì (r)	N	thing(s), affair(s)	033
148	试	shì	V	to try	053
149	售货员	shòuhuòyuán	N	shop assistant, salesclerk	051
150	书	shū	N	book	051
151	刷	shuā	V	to brush	042
152	睡觉	shuì jiào	V//O	to sleep	042
153	随便	suíbiàn	Adj	random, casual	053
154	所以	suǒyǐ	Conj	therefore, so	042
T					
155	他	tā	Pr	he, him	021
156	她	tā	Pr	she, her	021
157	太	tài	Adv	too	031
158	天	tiān	N	day	031
159	挺	tǐng	Adv	very, rather	053
160	同事	tóngshì	N	colleague	033
161	同学	tóngxué	N	classmate	022
W					
162	外边	wàibian	N	outside	023

163	晚	wǎn	Adj	late	042
164	晚上	wǎnshang	N	night, evening	033
165	位	wèi	M	*a polite measure word for people*	021
166	我	wǒ	Pr	I, me	011
167	我们	wǒmen	Pr	we, us	021
168	五	wǔ	Nu	five	042

X

169	洗	xǐ	V	to wash	042
170	洗澡	xǐ zǎo	V∥O	to have a shower	042
171	下班	xià bān	V∥O	to get off work	043
172	下午	xiàwǔ	N	afternoon	041
173	先	xiān	Adv	first	042
174	现在	xiànzài	N	now	041
175	想	xiǎng	OpV	would like	051
176	小	xiǎo	Adj	small, little	051
177	小姐	xiǎojie	N	Miss, young lady	021
178	小时	xiǎoshí	N	hour	043
179	谢谢	xièxie	V	to thank	012
180	新	xīn	Adj	new	033
181	星期五	xīngqīwǔ	N	Friday	043
182	星期一	xīngqīyī	N	Monday	043
183	行	xíng	V	OK	033
184	姓	xìng	V/N	one's surname is... ; surname	012
185	休息	xiūxi	V	to have a rest	043
186	学生	xuésheng	N	student	031
187	学习	xuéxí	V	to learn, to study	031
188	学校	xuéxiào	N	school	023

Y

189	牙	yá	N	tooth	042
190	研讨会	yántǎohuì	N	seminar	041
191	要	yào	OpV	to want	051
192	要	yào	V	to need, to want	052
193	也	yě	Adv	too, also	011
194	一	yī	Nu	a, an, one	032
195	衣服	yīfu	N	clothes	053
196	一共	yígòng	Adv	in total	052
197	一下	yíxià	Q	*a quantifier used after a verb to indicate a short, quick, random or informal action*	022
198	以后	yǐhòu	N	after, later	042
199	以前	yǐqián	N	before, ago	043
200	一般	yìbān	Adv	usually	042
201	一点儿	yìdiǎnr	Nu	a little, a bit	052
202	英(语)	Yīng(yǔ)	N	English	051
203	邮件	yóujiàn	N	email	033
204	邮箱	yóuxiāng	N	mailbox, email address	032
205	有	yǒu	V	to have	011
206	有点儿	yǒudiǎnr	Adv	a bit, a little	053
207	有时候	yǒushíhou	Adv	sometimes	042
208	又…… 又……	yòu…… yòu……		both…and…	051

Z

209	再	zài	Adv	again, once more	053
210	再见	zàijiàn	V	goodbye	012
211	在	zài	Prep	at, in, on	023
212	咱们	zánmen	Pr	we, us	041

213	早	zǎo	Adj	early	042
214	早饭	zǎofàn	N	breakfast	042
215	怎么	zěnme	QPr	how	012
216	怎么样	zěnmeyàng	QPr	what about	051
217	找	zhǎo	V	to look for	051
218	找	zhǎo	V	to give change	052
219	这	zhè	Pr	this	011
220	真	zhēn	Adv	really	033
221	知道	zhīdào	V	to know	041
222	中文	Zhōngwén	N	Chinese language	011
223	中午	zhōngwǔ	N	noon	043
224	周末	zhōumò	N	weekend	043
225	住	zhù	V	to live, to stay, to dwell	023
226	准备	zhǔnbèi	V	to prepare	041
227	走	zǒu	V	to walk	041
228	最近	zuìjìn	Adv	recently, lately	033
229	左右	zuǒyòu	N	about, around	042
230	作业	zuòyè	N	homework	042

专有名词
Proper Nouns

B				
1	北京	Běijīng	Beijing, the capital of China	012
D				
2	德国	Déguó	Germany	011
3	对外经济贸易大学	Duìwài Jīngjì Màoyì Dàxué	University of International Business and Economics (UIBE)	031
F				
4	法国	Fǎguó	France	021
J				
5	经贸大学	Jīngmào Dàxué	the abbreviation of UIBE	031
K				
6	卡尔	Kǎ'ěr	a person's name	011
7	康	Kāng	a surname	012
8	康爱丽	Kāng Àilì	a person's name	011
L				
9	李	Lǐ	a surname	022
M				
10	明明	Míngming	a Chinese student's given name	022
O				
11	欧洲	Ōuzhōu	Europe	021

S				
12	上海	Shànghǎi	Shanghai, one of the largest cities in China	022
W				
13	王	Wáng	a surname	012
Z				
14	中国	Zhōngguó	China	021